CW00487180

# Rediscovering a
## Ministry of Health

# Rediscovering a
## Ministry of Health

Parish Nursing as a Mission of the Local Church

HELEN ANNE WORDSWORTH

WIPF & STOCK · Eugene, Oregon

REDISCOVERING A MINISTRY OF HEALTH
Parish Nursing as a Mission of the Local Church

Copyright © 2015 Helen Anne Wordsworth. All rights reserved. Except for brief quotations in critical publications or reviews, no part of this book may be reproduced in any manner without prior written permission from the publisher. Write: Permissions, Wipf and Stock Publishers, 199 W. 8th Ave., Suite 3, Eugene, OR 97401.

Wipf & Stock
An Imprint of Wipf and Stock Publishers
199 W. 8th Ave., Suite 3
Eugene, OR 97401

www.wipfandstock.com

ISBN 13: 978-1-4982-0595-5

Manufactured in the U.S.A.

All Scripture quotations are taken from the New International Version of the Bible.

This book is dedicated with love to Robert, Anna and Paul, and to all the UK parish nurses without whom it would not have been written.

# Contents

*List of Tables and Figures* | viii

*Preface* | xi

*Acknowledgments* | xiii

*Abbreviations* | xiv

1  Introduction | 1

2  Parish Nursing: A Developing Ministry | 19

3  Towards an Understanding of the Mission of an English Church | 42

4  Identification of a Method to Address the Research Question | 72

5  Findings Relating to the Fifteen Parish Nurse Churches | 93

6  Comparisons with the Control Group | 129

7  Significance of the Findings | 149

8  Rediscovering a Ministry of Health | 167

**Appendices**

1  Letter of Introduction | 173

2  Pre-interview Survey Sent to Ministers | 174

3  Semi-structured Interview Questions: Ministers | 180

4  Semi-structured Interview Questions: Nurses | 182

5  Interventions by Category | 184

*Bibliography* | 187

# Tables and Figures

TABLE 1    A framework for the writing up of the research | 94

FIGURE 1    Data drawn from interview transcripts:
volunteering | 96

FIGURE 2    Ministers' pre-interview survey question C2: the number
of people volunteering has increased | 98

FIGURE 3    Ministers' pre-interview survey question B62: parish
nurse involvement in volunteer coordination | 100

FIGURE 4    Ministers' pre-interview survey question B63: parish
nurse involvement in volunteer support | 101

FIGURE 5    Physical health interventions by churches with parish
nurses | 105

FIGURE 6    Mental health interventions by churches with parish
nurses | 108

FIGURE 7    Community health interventions by churches with parish
nurses | 111

FIGURE 8    Spiritual health interventions by churches with parish
nurses | 114

FIGURE 9    Ministers' pre-interview survey question C4ii: I have seen
spiritual growth in people who do not normally attend
church | 117

FIGURE 10    Ministers' pre-interview survey question C4i: I have
seen spiritual growth in people who normally attend
church | 118

**FIGURE 11**  Ministers' pre-interview survey question C5: people have to come to faith partly as a result of parish nurse interventions | 119

**FIGURE 12**  Ministers' pre-interview survey question C6: people have joined the church partly as a result of parish nurse interventions | 120

**FIGURE 13**  Interview responses: working with people in a way that respects freewill and choice | 122

**FIGURE 14**  Interview responses: integration of faith with parish nursing | 127

**FIGURE 15**  Ministers' pre-interview survey question C11: I recommend that other churches appoint parish nurses to enhance their mission involvement

**FIGURE 16**  Control group survey question B62, B63: volunteer coordination and support | 132

**FIGURE 17**  Control group survey: percentage of churches involved in physical health interventions compared with parish nurse churches | 135

**FIGURE 18**  Control group survey: percentage of churches engaged in mental health interventions compared with parish nurse churches | 136

**FIGURE 19**  Control group survey: percentage of churches engaged in community health interventions compared with parish nurse churches | 138

**FIGURE 20**  Control group survey: percentage of churches engaged in spiritual health interventions compared with parish nurse churches | 140

**FIGURE 21**  Control group survey: interventions as a percentage of total possible interventions | 141

**FIGURE 22**  Average church time spent with non-church people by denomination | 143

**FIGURE 23**  Average church time spent with non-church people by context of church | 144

# Preface

PARISH NURSING MINISTRY COMMENCED in the UK in November 2003. It involves the appointment of a registered nurse as part of the church ministry team, to work on behalf of the church, developing a whole-person health program with both congregation and community.

This initiative is not simply a pragmatic approach to filling gaps in health care provision. It is deeply founded on a Judeo-Christian understanding of healing and wholeness, and the gospel imperative to share God's offer of life in all its fullness with all people groups. The reason for writing this book is to present some evidence that will help churches and nurses understand just how much the work of Parish nursing enhances the mission of the local church.

I am grateful that Wipf and Stock Publishers agreed to publish this work. Some minor changes have been made to the original thesis, but as practical theology it was originally written in a way that I hope is accessible to nurses as well as church leaders and mission enablers. Most of all, I hope that it will encourage more churches to take up health ministry as authentic mission.

Helen Wordsworth
Peterborough, UK
October 2014

# Acknowledgments

I OWE SINCERE GRATITUDE to all those who have taken part in this research and especially to the fifteen ministers and their fifteen parish nurses who gave interviews. Much appreciation is due to the academic staff at Spurgeon's College who patiently assisted the development of this study and especially to Revd. Dr. Derek Tidball for his helpful accompaniment in the research and the writing up of this work.

I am also grateful to the Revd. Geoff Colmer and the trustees of the Central Baptist Association for their encouragement in this research; to Dr. Malcolm Rigler and my colleagues on the Council of Reference (formerly the Steering Group) for Parish Nursing Ministries UK; and to the past and present trustees, and staff, without whom this initiative would not have taken root in Britain.

At the time of writing there are ninety-two parish nurses engaged in health-related mission on behalf of churches in the UK and I have learned much from all of them as we have worked together to rediscover this aspect of missional activity. In addition, I am indebted to my friends in parish nursing around the world, particularly Professor Ann Solari-Twadell, and Revd. Dr. Deborah Patterson.

And finally to my husband Rob, daughter Anna, and son Paul, who have been my constant supporters and wise advisers throughout the implementation and evaluation of parish nursing in the UK.

# Abbreviations

| | |
|---|---|
| DAWN | Disciple A Whole Nation |
| GP | General Practitioner |
| MS | Multiple Sclerosis |
| NHS | National Health Service |
| NIC | Nursing Interventions Classification |
| NMC | Nursing and Midwifery Council |
| PNMUK | Parish Nursing Ministries UK |
| PN | Parish Nurse |
| TEAR Fund | The Evangelical Alliance Relief Fund |
| UK | United Kingdom |
| US | United States of America |

# 1

# Introduction

PARISH NURSING IS DEFINED as "the intentional integration of the practice of faith with the practice of nursing so that people can achieve wholeness in, with, and through the community of faith in which parish nurses serve."[1] It may also be known as "Faith Community nursing,"[2] and sometimes "Congregational nursing," "Church nursing," or "Pastoral nursing." In its contemporary form, parish nursing began in Chicago in 1985 with six pilot nurses; there are now around twelve thousand trained parish nurses in twenty-three countries across the world.

Revd. Dr. Deborah Patterson was Executive Director of the International Parish Nurse Resource Centre when it was based in Saint Louis, Missouri. She notes that interest in and research work around this topic is spreading.[3] However, much of the academic research so far is in the US, and relates to the application of the practice to the physical health of clients. Very little research has so far been done elsewhere, and there has been no

1. Patterson, *Health Ministries*, 34. This definition was debated and agreed by six hundred parish nurses gathered at the Westberg symposium in Chicago in October 2000.

2. The use of the term Parish in the UK is often associated with the Church of England, but it also has a civic meaning. It should be noted that the Lutheran church, the Church of Scotland and the Catholic church are also divided into (differing) parishes. In Australia and New Zealand, the American Nursing Association's term Faith Community Nurse is preferred. However this denotes a degree of exclusivity by religion and since people of any faith may access the services of a Parish nurse, the preferred generic term in the UK is "Parish nurse."

3. Ibid., 23.

attention specifically given to any mission potential that might be connected with the appointment of a parish nurse in a local church.

As a regional minister/mission enabler in the Central Association of the Baptist Union of Great Britain, a major part of my ministry was to explore with churches in four counties of England the theological foundation, contextual relevance and effectiveness of various mission initiatives that may help them reach out to the communities in which they are placed, or with which they engage. My background in nursing and community health, together with my growing conviction that the gospel value of wholeness includes both physical and spiritual aspects of health, has often led me to consider whether or not there might be a role for a local church in health ministry. Throughout its history, the National Health Service has hired church premises for child health clinics and occasionally commissioned third sector organizations to provide volunteer services to augment primary care, but in the light of recent government proposals to involve charities in the development of the "Big Society" this issue has become more prominent.[4] Some churches have seen this as an opportunity to engage more readily with the community. Others have shown some reticence, fearing that the contribution of churches may become a substitute for community services that should be provided by the government.

Health ministry began to be promoted as far back as the 1960s; one of the recommendations of the Tübingen consultations, set up by the World Council of Churches in 1964 and 1967 was that the local church should be the primary agent for healing, even with the legitimate existence of specialized Christian institutions like hospitals, primary health services and special healing homes.[5]

In September 2000, developments in parish nursing in the US were brought to my attention, and I began to investigate this topic from a theological perspective. My interest resulted in the writing of a dissertation for a Masters degree in Applied Theology.[6] This sought to offer theological reflections on whether parish nursing was an appropriate mission opportunity for churches in England. In order to address that question, the following areas were investigated:

---

4. Cameron, "Transcript of a Speech," lines 13–23.
5. World Council of Churches, "Healing Mission," 8.
6. Wordsworth, "Parish Nursing."

- the practice of parish nursing as it stood then in America, Canada, and Australia;
- the historical and philosophical roots of the movement;
- a Biblically-based theology of health;
- the context for missional activity in England;
- current national health service objectives and needs from a nursing perspective.

I conducted a literature search including textbooks and papers that had been written around the principles and practice of parish nursing; theological approaches to health; missiology; and papers from the UK government's Department of Health.

The conclusions of that earlier study were firstly that although both the church and health contexts in England were completely different from those observed in the US, there were core values and principles in the theory and practice of parish nursing that could be appropriate for English churches; and secondly, that such an initiative might sit well with the churches' concern for wholistic mission alongside the current national interest in spiritual care.[7] I listed some recommendations for further work. These included further UK conferences, the consideration of different terminology for a UK context, the need to disseminate information at all levels of church and health service life, the setting up of pilot studies, the establishment of a resource for delivery, funding and support, and the need to contribute to the body of knowledge that was beginning to grow around the practice.

Eight years after the first work was completed, these recommendations had all been followed through: I had been encouraged both by tutors and by the chief nurse at the Department of Health to develop seven pilot projects in the UK. The results of these pilots and subsequent projects had prompted me to begin an initiative to promote parish nursing in the UK as a part of enabling churches in mission. This included the founding and development of a new charity, "Parish Nursing Ministries UK," which now provides training and coordination for parish nurses in more than eighty churches of different denominations in England, Scotland, and Wales.

7. The word "holistic" is spelled "wholistic" throughout this book, in recognition of a decision by the International Parish Nurse Resource Centre in 2008 to adopt the "w" in order to distinguish whole-person care from the use of the word holistic in conjunction with new-age or alternative therapies.

Nurses in both Germany and Kenya had begun parish nurse programs in their own countries as a direct result of the work here in the UK. Interest from both churches and nurses was continuing to grow, basic training courses were being offered twice yearly, and a new Masters level module "Exploring Parish Nursing," validated by the University of Chester, was delivered for the first time in 2010. A varied research program around parish nursing that began in the US was now beginning to develop in other countries and in the UK. It was now time to evaluate the initiative.

The UK charity's mission statement is as follows:

> Parish Nursing Ministries UK will develop and promote the concept, standards and scope of practice, and implementation of parish nursing within the UK, thereby enabling Christian denominations and churches to express their whole person health ministries with individuals and communities.[8]

This has been done first by creating interest at local church level, then recruiting, training, and resourcing Christians who are registered nurses with community experience to work as part of a church's ministry team in a voluntary or paid capacity. These "Parish" nurses seek to lead a team of church volunteers in a wholistic health ministry that complements state provision and offers spiritual support as core to practice. My earlier work had established the appropriateness of the ministry of parish nursing for English churches. This book describes a research dissertation that set out to ascertain whether or not parish nursing has made a difference to the mission of local churches, and if so, how this has happened.

Such a study has begun the process of establishing an academically rigorous UK contribution to the body of knowledge around parish nursing that will inform and improve future development both in the UK and beyond.

It may help to discern ways forward for the ongoing implementation of parish nursing in the UK, with particular application for ministers and mission enablers as they seek to increase the outreach of the churches; the charity and its regional coordinators as they support this; theological colleges and denominations as they review ministry training and recognition processes for parish nurses; and primary health-care teams as they consider the contribution that churches may make to the health of a local community.

8. From the 2005 business plan, Parish Nursing Ministries UK. The charity was registered in November 2005 and officially launched at its first symposium in 2006 at Hothorpe Hall, Leicestershire. In 2013 it had ten part-time regional coordinators, a part-time communications resourcing and development officer, and a part-time finance officer.

## AREAS OF INFLUENCE OF PARISH NURSING

The scope of the ministry of parish nursing will be described in more detail in chapter two. It claims to have an effect in three areas of influence by encouraging[9]

- nurses to reclaim the spiritual dimension of health care;
- health care systems to treat the patient as a whole;
- churches to restore the health and healing mission of the gospel.

My work in enabling churches in mission resounded clearly with the third of these aims and it was this that first led me to explore parish nursing in 2001. But my background in nursing has also awakened much interest in the first two of these aims, and since they are not unrelated to the mission of the church, they deserve to be discussed alongside the third aim.

### The ministry of parish nursing aims to reclaim the spiritual dimension of health care:

Florence Nightingale embarked upon her task to reform the practice of nursing with a strong sense of vocation from God.[10] Many healthcare institutions were started by monks, nuns, or people who had a sense of the spiritual dimension of health. Most hospitals have since been absorbed into the National Health Service (NHS), and although there is recognition that a patient's religious and cultural needs should be addressed, this is largely done through the office of chaplaincy.[11] Nurses who have applied for introductory training as a UK parish nurse frequently refer to a sense of divine calling to nursing in the first instance, and subsequently to parish nursing. Yet in their application forms they write of frustration in not being able to give their time to spiritual care within the NHS and of a desire to use their skills through the church so that they may offer people more time and attend more closely to spiritual needs. In the nursing context, despite laudable intentions, spiritual care has sometimes been reduced to the identification of a patient's religion so that the appropriate end-of-life rituals or

---

9. Statement agreed at the Westberg Parish Nurse Symposium in Chicago, September 2000.

10. O'Brien, *Spirituality in Nursing*, 44.

11. Department of Health, *Your Guide to the NHS*, 29.

dietary requirements may be fulfilled. This seems to suggest that there is indeed a need to reclaim the spiritual dimension of healthcare in the UK.

Parish nursing claims to offer health promotion with a focus on the intentional care of the spirit. That raises the question of how to define the phrases "spiritual care" and "spiritual need," and that of whether or not the term "spirituality" should be adopted for those aspects of health that are hard to categorize in other ways. An examination of nursing literature databases demonstrates that there has been an increase in the prominence of spirituality as a subject for publication by nursing contributors since 1990.[12] And in recognition of the renewed interest in the subject, spiritual care has been addressed by special day conferences organized by the Royal College of Nursing, in April 2009 and 2011.

In 2000, Greasley et al. conducted a focus group study with service users, carers and mental health professionals in the NHS on the concept of spiritual care. They concluded that the subject was poorly understood but that it related to the acknowledgement of a person's sense of meaning and purpose to life which may or may not be linked to formal religious practice. It was also associated with the concept of interpersonal care, love and compassion.[13] Other definitions of spirituality include: "being in harmony with the Universe, and striving for answers about the infinite";[14] and "connectedness, within oneself, with others and the environment, with the unseen, God, or a power greater than oneself."[15] McSherry has brought together the offerings of a number of authors on defining spiritual need. He attempts to summarize them as follows: The need

- for meaning and purpose
- for love and harmonious relationships
- for forgiveness
- for a source of hope and strength
- for creativity
- for trust
- for the ability to express one's own beliefs and values
- to maintain spiritual practices

12. Gilliat-Ray, "Nursing, Professionalism, and Spirituality," 335–49.
13. Greasley et al., "Concept of Spiritual Care," 629–37.
14. Murray and Zentner, *Nursing Concepts,* 259.
15. Reed, "Emerging Paradigm," 350.

- to express ones' own belief in God or deity (for some individuals)[16]

But John Paley has challenged the use of the term "spirituality" in a series of articles offering a reductionist view.[17] He draws from a variety of contributors on the subject and notes that the word has come to embrace a wide variety of diverse practices and personal preferences:

> Henceforward, spirituality becomes detached from its historical associations with mysticism, contemplation, discipline, and piety, circumscribed by a determinate system of beliefs, practices and ritual. Free of these constraints, it is transformed into a sort of giant conceptual sponge, absorbing a lavish and apparently inexhaustible range of items: humanistic psychology, Jungianism, borrowings from the Tao, Vedanta and Buddhism; complementary therapies, ecological concerns, astrology, tarot, bodywork; the appreciation of art, poetry and music, the contemplation of nature; personal wellbeing, relationships, hope, the search for meaning and purpose, one's highest values, political ideals, work, physical activity, personal gain; ideas about unity, energy, connectedness, transcendence, and many more.[18]

Paley's argument is illustrated by the approach of Heelas and Woodhead in their research on religion in relation to spirituality; they include many of the above categories in their attempt to compare activities linked to alternative spiritualities with religious attendance in Kendal.[19] Clarke also offers a critique of the ways in which nurses have tried to define spirituality: She concludes that the model often used is "too large, too existential and too inclusive to be manageable in practice without being indistinguishable from psycho-social care," and asks whether there might be "a more practical and user-friendly way to incorporate spirituality in practice."[20]

Swinton and Pattison have argued that spiritual care is not a coherent entity, being about absence rather than presence—the gaps in care rather than the certainties of it.[21] They emphasize the value of seeing spiritual care

---

16. McSherry, *Making Sense of Spirituality*, 56–57.
17. Paley, "Spirituality and Nursing," 3–18.
18. Ibid., 5.
19. Heelas and Woodhead, *Spiritual Revolution*, 23–30.
20. Clarke, "Critical View," 1666–73.
21. Swinton and Pattison, "Moving Beyond Clarity," 226–37.

as a vague concept, not necessarily subject to the multitude of measurable outcomes that characterize physical care.

The difference between the UK and US cultural backgrounds has relevance in this discussion. It should be recognized that American authors have been writing from a context in which considerably more people attended regular religious services than people in the UK over the same period. Burkhart and Solari-Twadell quote Teilhard de Chardin, a philosopher who suggested that spirituality was "the ability to search for meaning and purpose in life."[22] They note many other contributions, including the spirit as "the relationship between mind and body, freedom of choice, connecting with self and others, with art, music, literature and nature, and with a higher power through prayer or meditation."[23] They found that the literature on spirituality defined it as the broader concept, with religiousness (being more closely related to a faith community or a social institution) as a subset of it. They note that some American religious contributors saw things the other way round, religion being the broader concept, and spirituality a subset of it. But they suggest that both spirituality and religiousness should be seen as two separate but related concepts and that each had a place in nursing diagnosis.

O'Brien, also from the North American context, offers a spiritual assessment scale, structured around personal faith, religious practice and spiritual contentment. She describes ways in which, for those of various faiths, spiritual care may also mean the facilitation of meaningful religious practice, or the accessibility of aids for prayer.[24]

Christian spiritual care is based on an understanding of the theology of the Holy Spirit and his work in the life of the world and the believer. It is modeled on the ministry of Jesus and includes such Biblical concepts as love, faith, salvation, eternal hope, forgiveness, healing, reconciliation, freedom, discipleship, perseverance, enabling, belonging, peace, giving, and prayer. Jesus' teaching on judgment, the need to choose to follow God's will, and the discomfort that this may sometimes bring is also part of a Christian approach to spirituality. Paul writes that "the fruit of the Spirit is love, joy, peace, patience, kindness, goodness, faithfulness, gentleness, self-control."[25] Whilst these may all sound excellent objectives, the attainment

22. Burkhart and Solari-Twadell, "Spirituality and Religiousness," 47.

23. Ibid., 48–54.

24. O'Brien, *Spirituality in Nursing*, 58–62.

25. Galatians 5:22–23

of them will require diligence and even pain. Some, but perhaps not all of these spiritual attributes will be recognized as desirable by those of other faiths or no faith, or those who hold Christian faith without attending a place of worship. However, this perspective of spirituality from a Christian point of view differs significantly from the more vague definitions that can be found in some of the English literature.

There is considerable discourse about whether or not the spiritual dimension of health care could or should be reclaimed in general by nurses in the UK and this will be explored further towards the end of chapter two. But some agreement exists around the idea that at least for some patients and clients, attention to issues of meaning, purpose, hope, and relationship to God and others is important, whether or not it is classed as spirituality and whether or not it reflects a Christian perspective.

## The ministry of parish nursing aims to treat the patient as a whole person:

Foundational to the development of parish nursing is a Judeo-Christian view of personhood as an integrated whole, a perspective of human entity which will be discussed further in chapter 3. Medical models focus largely on the treatment with drugs or surgery of particular physical or mental diseases. Parish nurses are not alone in seeking a more wholistic approach to health-care. The House of Lords Report on Complementary and Alternative Medicine lists three groups of alternative practitioners: Group one includes the commonly recognized five disciplines: homeopathy, osteopathy, chiropractic, acupuncture, and herbal medicine. Group two focuses on complementary treatments that do not claim to be diagnostic: for example, aromatherapy, massage, counseling, stress therapy, meditation and healing. Group three covers others such as Chinese medicine and crystal therapy.[26] Suitably qualified parish nurses sometimes offer treatments from group two and may refer people to recognized practitioners in group one. So there is some overlap. Like some of these complementary therapies, parish nursing challenges organizations to address the spiritual needs of patients as well as physical and mental needs. For example, the World Health Organization's current definition of health is "A state of complete physical, mental and

26. NHSTA Directory of Complementary and Alternative Practitioners. http://www. nhsdirectory.org.

social well-being and not merely the absence of disease or infirmity."[27] This has not changed since 1948, despite suggestions from various professional sources, including complementary and alternative medicine practitioners, that the concepts of "emotional" or "spiritual" health should be included. Canadian parish nurses have been part of a campaign to see that the words "and spiritual" are included before "wellbeing."[28] The reason they have been given for not changing the definition is that in Africa and parts of South America, the influence of the witch-doctor over health is still very strong, and to include the word "spiritual" would give authority to such practitioners. In the UK, the Health Education Authority of 1997 acknowledged spirituality as part of a wider definition of mental health, although as has been seen, the concept is not without controversy.[29]

Whole-person care, wholistic or holistic care means that no one aspect of health is treated without reference to the whole. Holism derives from *holos*, which means whole. McSherry defines holism as meaning that "no system, biological, psychosocial, spiritual or environmental can be viewed in isolation because they all make up the whole person."[30] Therefore any attempt by medical staff to treat the physical needs of a person without thinking about their mental health, social need, or environmental conditions would be contrary to wholistic principles. But some organizations or churches might focus on the spiritual needs of a person without reference to their physical, mental, social, or environmental needs. That too would contravene wholistic principles.

It might be argued that patients in hospital, hospice care, and mental health services do currently have access to whole-person care. In addition to potential referral to various specialists in mental or physical health, they may be directed towards health care chaplaincy and chaplaincy volunteers. But health care is not solely confined to institutional work. Most patients, even if hospitalized, spend very little time under the care of a hospital. At any one time the number of inpatients represents a very small percentage of those who are experiencing health needs. Most are treated by General Practitioners, who have very little time to deal with some of the "spiritual" needs of their patients, and may also feel unable to address some of the mental, social, and environmental problems that present to them on a daily basis.

27. World Health Organization, "Definition of Health."
28. This campaign has not yet succeeded in bringing change to the definition.
29. Health Education Authority, *Mental Health Promotion.*
30. McSherry, "Making Sense of Spirituality," 74.

There is a movement towards the appointment of chaplains at GP surgeries. While this is to be welcomed, it is not currently a common practice and is somewhat restricted by funds available.[31] It does not normally include the deployment of a volunteer team unless an accompanying charity is in place, and it may only be accessible to the patients that are currently registered with a particular surgery.

Should NHS-funded community nurses therefore be encouraged to identify spiritual or psycho-social need and make appropriate interventions or referrals? There is considerable concern about this, not least because there is doubt that nurses have the right experience or training to deal with these issues, and nurses are only allowed to intervene to the level of their competence. There have been isolated media reports of NHS-employed nurses being disciplined for talking about faith or offering prayer as part of their work.[32] Caroline Petrie was working as a community nurse when she visited an elderly patient and after treating her, asked if she would like her prayer for her recovery. The patient declined and nothing more was said, although the patient reported this comment to the next nurse, who reported it to her manager. Caroline was suspended on grounds that she had acted against the NMC code of practice. However, that code did not prohibit prayer if it was in the interests of the patient, and did not lay down specific rules about what may and may not be done in relation to prayer. Caroline was re-instated. A survey followed, led by the Nursing Times in which 91 percent of the 2,500 respondents felt that Caroline had not contravened the code and should not have been suspended. The Trust stated that in the case of their employed staff, a request for prayer should be initiated by the patient and not by the nurse. More guidance was called for in making spiritual assessments and discussing matters of faith and prayer.[33] The latest NHS guidelines give more clarity on equality and diversity issues, and warn against the practice of proselytization, but do not fully address the spiritual elements in a whole-person assessment and care planning process.[34]

In the delivery of health care, adequate evidence as a rationale for interventions is required. Nursing and medical research is often derived from quantitative, double-blind controlled research methods whereas spiritual

31. This movement is represented by the Professional Association of Community Healthcare Chaplaincy, formed in March 2011.

32. Alderson, "Nurse Suspended."

33. "Christian Nurse Suspended."

34. Department of Health, "Religion or Belief."

care in nursing can be examined more effectively in qualitative ways. Swinton and Mowat note that qualitative research is often caricatured as anecdotal and lacking in rigor.[35] Yet in recent years the number of qualitative studies in both nursing and applied theology has grown. If the patient is to be treated as a whole person, there is a need for more research to underpin the spiritual elements of care. Perhaps the knowledge base that is built as a result of careful and creative research methods by parish nurses could contribute to a wider range of evaluative tools for assessing the delivery and/or effect of spiritual care. If this happens, health care systems may be encouraged to take spiritual care more seriously. One example of such potential may be seen in a three-year study from California where the spiritual care interventions of ten parish nurses were explored using a grounded theory method.[36] It would be interesting to see if this methodology can be demonstrated in a more secular European context, and whether the outcomes would be similar.

In treating the patient as a whole person, parish nursing advocates the raising of standards of health care for all, regardless of race, gender, religion, or ability to pay. Although not unique to Christian values, this may happen at an individual or community level, and derives from a Biblical perspective on justice. It encourages the building of relationships between health service providers and churches so that care offered to patients of the health service may include referral, where appropriate, to an adequately qualified faith-based group or specialist, where spiritual care may be offered alongside physical care. Since this kind of referral is optional, the client or patient decides whether or not to receive it or continue with it.

## The ministry of parish nursing aims to restore the health and healing mission of the gospel:

Parish nursing is founded on the belief that if salvation is for the whole person then the local church should be involved in wholistic health care as part of its mission. This assumption will be explored further in chapter 3. Many Christian health care professionals will act on this conviction by choosing to work solely in the state or private health service, but if this is the church's expression of its mission, then these individuals will still need to be supported at least in prayer by the church.

35. Swinton and Mowat, *Practical Theology*, 31.
36. Van Dover and Pfeiffer, "Spiritual Care," 213–21.

In following the Biblical principles of justice, respect, and righteousness, parish nursing also advocates the upholding of professional standards of accountability, record-keeping, referral, respect for a person's faith position, patient choice, and confidentiality wherever care is offered. Where a client is experiencing injustice affecting their health, a parish nurse may work with them to help them confront that problem.

Most churches see pastoral care and prayer for those who are sick as a routine part of a minister's job description or that of a pastoral care committee. Some have professional counseling or social work teams as well. Parish nursing seeks to enhance this by facilitating or taking part in different forms of healing prayer, providing follow-up if required, and being a resource to pastoral workers when it comes to knowledge of disease, health systems, and self-care.

Parish nursing seeks to improve the wellness of the congregation and community through health education programs and personal health advice. Members of churches and ministry teams are sometimes inhibited in their involvement in the work of God's Kingdom by their physical or mental health condition. If this may be improved by better self-care, nutritional attention, or health education then the church will be more able to participate in their mission task.[37] If everything has been done to achieve this, a parish nurse may help people to accept their limitations and still work towards helping others through them.

Parish nursing encourages volunteering. The role of the parish nurse in promotion, preparation for and coordination of volunteering should increase the capacity of the church to offer help to families and individuals with practical needs. Additionally, the opportunity to serve may provide a sense of identity and usefulness for those clients who do not attend church but who seek a greater sense of purpose in their lives.

Perhaps more significantly for a UK context where in 2005—6.3 percent of the population regularly attended church[38]—than for the US where the average figure was 44 percent,[39] parish nursing ministry aims to extend the health ministry as described above into the community. This may happen through friends and neighbors of those who use church buildings, or referrals from chaplains or general practitioners. People that neither attend church nor have a strong faith may therefore experience the health and

37. Adams, "Nurses in Churches," 16–17.
38. Brierley, *Pulling out of the Nosedive*, 12.
39. Gallup, "Church Attendance USA."

healing ministry of the gospel unconditionally; that is, they may receive help without being persuaded to change their faith position or join a particular organization. Unruh and Sider, in a comprehensive study of the mission programs of fifteen socially active churches in Philadelphia, examine the ways in which congregations may serve society, with particular attention to the faith element involved. They classify the social ministry programs of these churches in a typology of religious characteristics that range from secular, where there is no religious content in the social service provided, to faith-secular partnership, to faith background, to faith affiliated, to faith centered, and finally to faith-permeated, where the service is offered in an explicitly religious way.[40] This typology is useful in that it helps both churches and funding organizations to identify the nature of the faith-sharing element in their social action programs. Even if service is offered at the secular end of this typology, where there is no reference to prayer or faith, the act of serving itself should result in the building of relational bridges with other voluntary organizations and individuals so that the church may increase its profile in community life. It may also help churches to rethink their role and strategy in God's mission.

Parish nursing is founded on the teaching of Jesus and aims to reconnect people with each other and with God. In recognition that the journey of faith is sometimes a long and difficult one, parish nurses are not taught to preach at clients but rather to seek to walk alongside them, as invited to do so. Parish nursing includes spiritual care as part of health care. Parish nurses employed or appointed by the church for their parish nursing hours may therefore provide resources, pray, or signpost to others about questions of faith when that is requested, and will include spiritual issues in their assessment of the care that is needed. Care must be taken to ensure that the client knows what organization the nurse represents. The Nursing and Midwifery Council's code of practice demands that nurses should always have respect for any decision the client may make, and this applies to spiritual care as much as to physical care.[41]

## THEOLOGICAL FOUNDATIONS

Each of these three areas of anticipated influence has an underlying theological imperative. For example, the Biblical theme of a divine calling

40. Unruh and Sider, *Saving Souls*, 110.
41. "Code of Practice."

connects with the sense of there being a spiritual dimension to health care; the Judeo-Christian theme of health as wholeness is the background to the idea of treating the patient as a whole person; the missiological theme of the extension of God's Kingdom through the church is the rationale for reclaiming the health and healing aspects of the gospel. By examining these themes in the light of theological literature I will argue in chapter three that each of these aims relate to what is known as *Missio Dei*, the mission of God. Thereby I will open up the possibility that parish nursing has the potential to help the church fulfill the mission of God.

## THE RESEARCH

For the first two of the aims referred to above, the time-span covered may not have been long enough to collect any significant amount of data. But there has now been enough evidence to present an evaluation of the extent to which parish nursing has helped churches to reclaim the health and healing aspects of the gospel in those local churches that have had parish nursing projects up and running for at least eighteen months.

Chapter 4 will describe the methodology used. Chapter 5 will report the findings of the research. Chapter 6 will offer an analysis and discussion of the findings and chapter 7 will draw some conclusions, and implications. Chapter 8 will consist of a summary, some recommendations, and a statement of vision.

## Reasons for undertaking the research

As both a Mission Enabler for 150 churches and UK Coordinator for Parish nursing, I needed to stand back and examine my practice with academic rigor in order to identify priorities. There appeared to be very little work on the missional implications of parish nursing so far, even in the US and none in the UK. Experience so far has shown that churches and ministers need to be convinced of the theological and missiological rationale for parish nursing if it is to be welcomed with enthusiasm by the congregation and have any long term sustainability. Like some other ideas from abroad, there is a danger that it could be rejected as the latest ecclesiological fashion, as the "hobby" of an over-enthusiastic nurse in the church, as a pragmatic and politically right-wing answer to the demands of community involvement and the "Big Society" or as a fund-releasing activity. All of these reasons for making decisions could jeopardize the intrinsic missional value of a local church's parish nursing ministry and threaten the longer-term implementation of the movement.

Whether or not this work shows that parish nursing is making some kind of difference to the mission of a local church, it should contribute an essential element to the thinking of both mission enablers and churches as they consider future mission strategy. It will also inform parish nurse educators and coordinators about issues that need to be addressed in the training and support of parish nurses. And it will help the charity formed for the development of parish nursing in the UK to focus on appropriate evidence-based ways of communicating the value of the practice. It may also help to identify any further implications that would be useful to local churches as they seek to fulfill their mission.

## The Research Question

The objective of the research was to discover the degree to which there is any clear missional benefit to be gained by a local church in appointing a parish nurse. This should assist a church that may be thinking about making such an appointment. The research question therefore was:

> "How far does parish nursing make a difference to the mission of English churches?"

In order to explore this it has been necessary to define what is meant by the "mission of English churches" and "missional benefit." Does this mean more conversions, or an increase in church membership or attendance, or greater community engagement, or perhaps more active faith in the lives of those already committed to following Christ? Reference to Biblical and contemporary missiological thinking has been helpful in determining the criteria for measurement.

But it was first important to establish some clarity on the scope of work of a parish nurse. This was done by reviewing the literature so far available on the practice of parish nursing. I have then examined the theological themes that underlie the areas that parish nursing seeks to influence; and I have shown how those may relate to what is understood as the mission of the local church.

## Methodological approach

Having arrived at a working definition of the terms, I have sought to answer the research question by using a qualitative study with fifteen English churches, each of which has been involved in a parish nursing project for at least eighteen months.

All twenty-nine of those eligible by these criteria were contacted to ask if they would like to participate, and all of those who responded were part of the sample. By denomination these were mostly Anglican or Baptist, but this reflected the fact that 90 percent of churches that had appointed parish nurses by that time were also either Anglican or Baptist. A question relating to the theological stance of the church was not asked, but it became clear during the course of the interviews that at least four of the churches studied were "high" church or liberal in their theology. So the study was not limited to evangelical churches. But it should be noted that this research did not reflect the experience of parish nursing in other English protestant denominations, nor in the Roman Catholic church or Orthodox tradition. In the future the method could be repeated to include those denominations now that they have begun to make parish nurse appointments.

The qualitative work included the recording of separate interviews with the ministers of those churches and with the parish nurses concerned. The interviews were transcribed and analyzed for references to any comments that related to aspects of my working definition of local church mission. This was augmented by sending a pre-interview questionnaire to the ministers of those fifteen churches. The questionnaire asked ministers to tick the categories of intervention with which their church has been engaged over the previous eighteen months. In addition to this, and in order to achieve some comparisons, the same questionnaire was randomly distributed through Anglican, Baptist, and Free Evangelical networks both on paper and via the internet and has been completed by a self-generated sample of the ministers of seventy-seven churches without a parish nurse. The results of the questionnaires have been tabulated and matched against the information from the parish nurse churches in chapter 6. Further triangulation has been achieved by using data from the annual statistical returns of parish nurses in 2010, because they related to the same categories of intervention as the questionnaires. The research method was therefore mixed, comprising both qualitative and quantitative components.

These three sources of data have provided some kind of answer to the research question, although from a largely Anglican and Baptist perspective. The data has been analyzed using five missional criteria that have been developed from a study of the theological foundation for the mission of a local church outlined in chapter 3. The same criteria can also be used as an additional tool by mission-enablers in determining the nature and range of missional activities undertaken by any local church.

The ethical guidelines for research as published by the University of Wales at the commencement of the study were followed. Strict confidentiality was observed, both in the conduct of the interviews and recording of them. It was made clear that participation in the interviews was entirely optional. The requirement to submit the proposal to an ethics committee did not apply at the time because the subjects interviewed were not minors or patients and were not classed as vulnerable adults. Since that time the guidelines for most institutions have been changed, and any proposal to repeat the work would need to be processed through a research ethics board.

# 2

# Parish Nursing: A Developing Ministry

## THE HISTORY OF PARISH NURSING

PROTESTANT EUROPE APPEARS TO have been the place where parish nursing started; Zersen points to the Gemeinderschwestern of nineteenth century Germany as the predecessors of parish nursing, along with "Episcopal, Methodist and Lutheran sisters of the same period in the U.S."[1] Theodor Fliedner, a Lutheran pastor, opened the first deaconess training center in Kaiserswerth, Germany in 1836.[2] In the preface to her biography of Fliedner, Winkworth shows that even as early as 1568, there was a proposal to appoint women to the office of nurses for the congregation in the Lutheran church in Wesel.[3]

Boulton describes parish nurses as having had "a central role in the lives of the poor in London in the seventeenth century."[4] Although there is no specific mention of spiritual care, this role appears to have included care of the sick poor, orphans, pregnant women, and lunatics. References to parish nurses seem to diminish beyond the early eighteenth century, when it appears that their work was largely taken over by the workhouses.

1. Zersen, "Parish Nursing," 19–20.
2. Boulton, "Welfare Systems," 127–51.
3. Winkworth, *Life of Pastor Fliedner*, 23.
4. "History of the Kaiserswerth Diaconate."

The birth of nursing as a professional activity is often attributed to Florence Nightingale, daughter of a wealthy family who experienced a "call" to care for the sick and then to volunteer for service in the Crimea. Her passion for the improvement of nursing care was deeply related to her faith in God, her belief in the necessity of good public health, and to her study of statistics.[5] These elements, along with her conviction that God wanted people to work towards improving health as well as praying for him to intervene, feature strongly in the development of parish nursing, and her visits to Fliedner's Lutheran hospital at Kaiserswerth had a formative effect on her, introducing her to a Christian institution that "performed its service of humankind in a devout and serious manner."[6] It is not surprising therefore that many parish nurses see their work as rooted in Nightingale's philosophy.

Catholic roots of parish nursing may be traced to the Daughters of Charity of Vincent de Paul in seventeenth-century France,[7] and Catholic parish nurses in the US often work closely with local branches of the society of St Vincent de Paul today.

Records relating to the Baptist Deaconess movement in the Angus Library at Regents Park College, Oxford, contain pictures of Baptist deaconesses in the late nineteenth century. They had to be trained as nurses first before they could enter theological college, and they wore nurses' uniform in their work. This historical involvement of nurses in the Baptist churches in England has been of immense importance in the work to persuade congregations of the relevance of parish nursing for the mission of the church today, especially where there are older members of the congregation who recall anecdotal stories of these sisters and their good works.

The modern parish nursing movement commenced with the vision of Granger Westberg in 1986 following his experiments with wholistic health centers in Chicago in the 1960s. One nurse was assigned to each of six churches in Chicago in 1986. Training was first offered by way of in-service seminars and study days. Soon a basic preparation course for registered nurses was developed and offered in a number of American states largely from existing colleges of nursing. The total number of those practicing as parish nurses appointed by their churches is not known, but it is estimated as over ten thousand. These nurses work from a wide variety of main line

5. McDonald, *Florence Nightingale*, 8.
6. Ibid., 8.
7. Solari-Twadell et al, *Parish Nursing*, 11–16.

denominations—Lutheran, Catholic, and Episcopal being the most common appointments, Baptist and Pentecostal the least common. Some nurses work in churches that are not their own denomination.

The movement spread to Canada in 1992.[8] A Canadian national structure was proposed in 1998 and the Canadian Association for Parish Nursing Ministry was formed in 2001. In Australia, Dr Anne Van Loon undertook a PhD in spiritual care in 1996 and at the same time started the Australian Faith Community Nurses Association, which now has around 150 members. In turn, they helped to start the work in New Zealand in 2001, and the movement spread amongst Pacific Islanders.[9]

Since 1986, there has been an Annual Symposium for parish nurses, organized by the International Parish Nurse Resource Centre. It is held in the US, named after Granger Westberg and sponsored by his family. Until 2001 this was held in Chicago, but it then moved to St. Louis. In 2003 there were more nurses from other countries in attendance, and by 2004 it was proposed that a World Forum for parish nursing be established. The rationale for this was in recognition of the fact that the contextual application of the principles of parish nursing differed from one country to another, and that much could be learned and shared through this cross-cultural work. That body was constituted the very next day and now meets annually at the Westberg symposium and by internet communication the rest of the year. Twenty-five countries now have at least the beginnings of a parish nurse movement, and these include developing nations in all five continents. A monthly newsletter links these initiatives.[10] In 2012 the International Parish Nurse Resource Center moved to be part of the Church Health Center in Memphis, Tennessee, and the annual Westberg Symposium is currently held in Memphis.

## THE PHILOSOPHY OF PARISH NURSING

Phyllis Ann Solari-Twadell and Mary Ann McDermott edited the first textbook on parish nursing in 1999.[11] The textbook provides a description of the philosophical principles underlying the practice that were developed by Ryan, Berry, Griffin, and Reeves:

8. "Historical Overview."
9. Wearne, "Faith Community Nursing."
10. Daniels, "World Forum Newsletter."
11. Solari-Twadell and McDermott, *Parish Nursing*, 15.

a. The spiritual dimension is central to the practice. It also encompasses the physical, psychological, and social dimensions of nursing practice.

b. The parish nurse balances knowledge with skill, the sciences with theology and humanities, service with worship, and nursing care functions with pastoral care functions. The historic roots of the role are intertwined with those of monks, nuns, deacons and deaconesses, church nurses, traditional healers, and the nursing profession itself.

c. The focus of practice is the faith community and its ministry. The parish nurse, in collaboration with the pastoral staff and congregational members, participates in the ongoing transformation of the faith community into a source of health and healing. Through partnership with other community health resources, parish nursing fosters new and creative responses to health concerns.

d. Parish nursing interventions are designed to build on and strengthen the capacities of individuals, families, and congregations to understand and care for one another in the light of their relationship to God, faith traditions, themselves, and the broader society. The practice holds that all persons are sacred and must be treated with respect and dignity. In response to this belief, the parish nurse assists and empowers individuals to become more active partners in the management of their personal health resources.

e. The parish nurse understands health to be a dynamic process that embodies the spiritual, psychological, physical, and social dimensions of the person. Spiritual health is central to well-being and influences a person's entire being. Therefore, a sense of well-being and illness may occur simultaneously. Healing may exist in the absence of cure.[12]

Solari-Twadell comments that the emphasis on spiritual care in the first of these statements assumes that the nurse will have developed a degree of spiritual maturity, and that this will differentiate the practice from the traditional role of a community health nurse.[13] To some extent that will depend on the extent to which those entering parish nursing have been exposed to opportunities for spiritual growth themselves. Sir George

12. These principles were developed by the philosophy work group, then refined and endorsed by the first Educational Colloquium, Mundelein, IL, June 1994. In the last of these principles, cure is understood as complete absence of the physical or mental disease, whereas healing is seen as a wholistic and dynamic concept that may bring remission of symptoms and shalom but not necessarily cure.

13. Solari-Twadell and McDermott, *Parish Nursing*, 4.

Castledine, Professor and Consultant of Nursing at the Institute of Age-ing and Health in Birmingham, notes that in the National Health Service (NHS) there is a feeling that a patient's spiritual needs can be met by a generic model of chaplaincy; that is, one chaplain for any kind of faith.[14] He suggests that the limited evidence available contradicts this; rather, it implies that a person's religious needs should be met by someone of their own faith. He offers parish nursing as a way forward for the UK.

If the nurse is working from a faith community, she/he will exercise that spiritual care from the perspective of that denomination or faith. But she/he must do so within the guidelines of the code of practice for nurses. In the UK this is issued by the Nursing and Midwifery Council (NMC) and demands that nurses must act with respect and dignity toward their patients at all times.[15] Each NHS trust has its own additional guidelines for its own staff and these may preclude nurses from initiating any conversa-tion about faith or prayer. It is paramount therefore that clients and patients know that a parish nurse is not employed by the NHS for the hours she/he works as a parish nurse, but by a named local church, and that they have a choice as to whether or not to receive parish nursing care. This is empha-sized during the training of UK parish nurses.

The second principle illustrates the overlap that the parish nurse role may sometimes have with a variety of other pastoral and practical car-ers. Churches sometimes raise such potential duplication as an argument against the need for parish nursing. Bergquist and King looked at the early literature on parish nursing and extrapolated five broad categories as a framework for future nursing theory, research, and practice. They showed that this overlap can also be a strength; the nurse is able to bring various care providers together, to add the faith element to community nursing, and to add medical knowledge to the insights of the pastoral team.[16] Clark and Olson examined the nature of the collaborative working between pastor and parish nurse as together they served a (non-churched) family whose lives changed when a baby was born with Down syndrome.[17] But if this team-working strength is to be released, it is vital that other team mem-bers understand the role and encourage the nurse. This is well illustrated

14. Castledine, "Spiritual State," 803.
15. Nursing and Midwifery Council, "Code of Practice."
16. Bergquist and King, "Parish Nursing," 155–70.
17. Clark and Olson, "Partnership that Matters," 27–40.

in two contrasting cases described by Bokinskie and Kloster:[18] Two nurses attended the basic preparatory course, one encouraged by her pastor and health committee who saw this as part of their outreach strategy, the other from a sense of personal vocation, but little support from the pastor or the church. Two years later, both were still practicing in an unpaid capacity, but the first was working ten hours a week in an effective ministry and the second working sporadically against a background of resistance.

Research by Biddix[19], Anderson[20], Adams[21], and many other North American nurses clearly demonstrates that the focus for parish nursing in the US is largely on caring within the faith community itself. This could partly be due to the fact that faith communities in the US are large and contain a greater percentage of the population than churches in the UK. A larger client caseload within the church, reaches a larger proportion of the national population. Not to be overlooked however are the underlying ecclesiologies; the internal focus may be a reflection of the nature of the missiological views that determine the life of those congregations.

The fourth statement encompasses the sacredness of the individual and the need for self-care. Parish nurses spend much of their time educating for health and creating awareness of symptoms that may be early indicators of disease. Such a resource would seem to be a gift to health services that are financially struggling to meet the treatment requirements of those who have left it too late to seek help. Chesley has looked at the role of parish nurses in cancer prevention, noting that since lifestyle choices are associated with around 70 percent of all cancers, parish nurses are well placed to educate congregations in this regard.[22]

Self-care is an acknowledged priority in the NMC code of practice.[23] It is also encouraged in NHS guidelines.[24] But it can foster unnecessary concern amongst the "worried well," a term used by health professionals to denote those patients who present too often with minor symptoms and take up valuable time. This philosophical theme needs to be read alongside the work of Abigail Rian-Evans on the Biblical distinctives in understand-

18. Bokinskie and Kloster, "Effective Parish Nursing," 20–25.

19. Biddix and Brown, "Establishing a Parish Nursing Program," 72–75.

20. Anderson, "Delivery of Health Care," 117–28.

21. Adams, "Nurses in Churches," 16–17.

22. Chesley, "Parish Nursing," 5.

23. "Code of Practice."

24. *Self-care: A Real Choice.*

ing health.[25] She notes one of these to be that the primary goal is other's health, not our own.

The final principle concerns the theology of healing and orientates towards a middle path—a recognition that while the church is called to a ministry of healing, this does not necessarily mean instantaneous cure. Churches and individuals hold to a range of views on healing, from those promoted by Professor Gordon Scorer, who argued that the age of miracles belonged to the past, and that churches should leave anything to do with health care to the medical profession,[26] to the view that any Christian may be trained to offer prayer for the sick with the expectation of physical healing, as outlined by Wimber and Springer.[27] This topic is examined in depth in a Church of England report, *A Time to Heal*.[28] A range of views on the subject is explored and edited in debate form by Ernest Lucas.[29] The extent to which healing should be part of the church's mission will be discussed in the next chapter.

## THE PRACTICE OF PARISH NURSING

McDermott and Burke describe seven "functions" of a Parish nurse that have been adopted as a standard for parish nursing practice internationally. They are:

- integrator of faith and health;
- health educator;
- personal health counselor;
- referral agent;
- trainer of volunteers;
- developer of support groups;
- health advocate.

They further note that this role does not "embrace the medical model of care or invasive practices such as blood drawing, medical treatments or

25. Rian-Evans, *Redeeming Marketplace Medicine*, 67.
26. Scorer, *Healing*.
27. Wimber and Springer, *Power Healing*, 181–97.
28. Church of England, *A Time to Heal*.
29. Lucas et al, *Christian Healing*.

maintenance of intravenous products."[30] A parish nurse therefore does not resemble the stereotyped UK image of a nurse as a hospital staff member in uniform who administers drugs and dressings under doctor's orders. The role is more similar to that of a nurse practitioner, community nursing sister, or health visitor, whose additional training enables them to practice as an independent professional, assessing the health of patients, offering health advice, referring to other professionals, and evaluating interventions. Bickley explores the roles of a nurse and points out that she/he does not have a monopoly on caring amongst other professions. However, she argues that the nurse is often, particularly during periods of illness, in continuous attendance upon the patient and that she/he is well placed to anticipate needs and interpret them to other team members. In doing this, she continues:

> she/he can not only assess the need for those aspects of care that she/he can meet directly, delegate to less skilled workers, or advise family and friends about . . . but can coordinate the caring interventions of other professionals whose specialist expertise may complement her own.[31]

Such a definition of nursing takes into account the fact that the nurse is not always the provider of care, but rather the one who observes, assesses need and potential threat against a model of living, encourages self-care, searches for appropriate interventions, coordinates the care provision, measures the outcome and initiates re-assessment. This view encompasses the many expressions of nursing that exist both in community and hospital, and is the foundation on which the role of the parish nurse is based.

A body of research in the practice of parish nursing has been building over the last fifteen years, some of which has focused on the range of interventions made by parish nurses. The vast majority of this research comes from North America and so the different religious and health service contexts need to be borne in mind when reading these from a UK perspective.

## The Range of Interventions

In 1997, Weiss, Matheus, and Schank offered a descriptive study of the way in which eleven parish nurses in eleven faith communities in Milwaukee,

30. McDermott and Burke, "When the Population," 179–90.
31. Bickley, "Contribution of Nursing," 82.

Wisconsin, helped people to work towards the attainment of the American government's health objectives.[32] They retrospectively reviewed the monthly reports of the nurses, together with semi-structured interviews. Nine healthy living objectives were identified: blood pressure knowledge and control; weight loss practices; vigorous physical activity; breast self-examination; home fire safety; stress management; reduction of heart disease and stroke; reduction of child abuse; and the maintenance of activities of daily living in older people. The strategies used by the nurses to address these objectives were documented. The communities in the sample were diverse both ethnically and denominationally, but this research focused purely on the physical and educational interventions made by the nurses. It revealed that parish nurse activities contributed to the empowerment process and to the attainment of these objectives.

Scott and Sumner had a more wholistic approach to their research on the range of interventions.[33] The method used was a lengthy telephone questionnaire with the clients of sixty-three parish nurse projects in western Iowa. The results showed that 92 percent said they had healthier lifestyles as a result of the parish nurse interventions, around 90 percent had emotional needs met, but only 50 percent said they had discussed spiritual topics with the parish nurse. Of these, only half had mentioned God's presence, healing, or hope. But this may have been a consequence of the method. The conversations were conducted by eight different researchers so there may have been some variation in the way in which the questions were asked. And while there were fifty-four questions on physical health, and forty-seven about emotional care, there were only thirty-four about spiritual care. The authors commented that the spiritual care aspect of parish nursing needs to be developed more fully to include reading of scripture, praying with or for clients, and the laying on of hands.

In an effort to be more specific about the nature of spiritual care in Christian parish nursing, in 2007 Van Dover and Pfeiffer published the results of a grounded theory approach. This is a qualitative method, developed in 1967 by Glaser and Strauss, in which words and phrases used in interviews are analyzed to identify common concepts that lead to theoretical elements emerging directly from the data.[34] They interviewed ten parish nurses in the Midwest and South West of the US, recording all the

32. Weiss et al., "Health Care Delivery," 368–72.

33. Scott and Sumner, "How do Parish Nurses," 16–18.

34. Glaser and Strauss, *Discovery of Grounded Theory*.

interviews and transcribing them verbatim. From this data emerged a substantive theory they called "Bringing God near." This encompassed five sequential phases that they extracted from the transcripts: "Trusting God" (as a parish nurse); "Forming relationships with the client"; "Opening to God" (the moment of awareness of God coming into the encounter); "Activating or nurturing faith" (where prayer was the common denominator); and "Recognizing spiritual renewal or growth" (where positive changes in attitudes, emotions and faith were reported). In summary, they suggest that when parish nurses and patients focus on God, their perspectives are changed about what is happening and God's place in this, as well as their place in God's bigger picture.[35]

## The Age Range of Clients

Some of the research has focused on the parish nurse role in relation to older people. Rydholm looked at the work of forty parish nurses working with elderly clients in Minnesota. Using structured field notes as data, she found that 53 percent of the concerns addressed were psychosocial or spiritual, and 47 percent were physical or functional. Of eighteen hundred concerns that were addressed, spiritual distress accounted for 34 percent; care-giver stress, 9 percent; isolation, 10 percent; symptom disregard, 19 percent; self-care in illness, 11 percent; safety concerns, 13 percent; and lifestyle issues, 4 percent.[36]

Boland has examined the (largely secular) literature on the effectiveness of interventions in the encouragement of health-promoting behaviors in the elderly.[37] She suggests that there are inconsistencies in much of the reported research but that two significant factors keep appearing: social support and spiritual beliefs. She urges further research in both these areas and comments on the potential of parish nursing to address both these dimensions of care.

O'Brien reported on the way in which parish nurses meet the spiritual needs of older people nearing death.[38] Fifteen chronically ill older people in a US West Coast urban area were visited and interviewed, and their responses were analyzed using "Spiritual Wellbeing in Illness," an established

35. Van-Dover and Pfeiffer, "Spiritual Care," 213–21.
36. Rydholm, "Patient-focused Care," 47–60.
37. Boland, "Parish Nursing," 355–68.
38. O'Brien, "Parish Nursing," 28–33.

interpretative theory that she had developed in her previous research. Their parish nurse documentation records and journal memos were added to the data. Diagnoses made were spiritual alienation, anxiety, anger, loss, and lack of peace; interventions by a parish nurse involved sharing of prayer and scripture, spiritual presence, and pastoral counseling. All clients responded well to the interventions made. However, it should be noted that all but one were already church members.

At the other end of life, Buijs and Olson have explored how, in various research literature, the two health determinants of social support and healthy child development are linked and have suggested that they could therefore be influenced by the work of parish nurses.[39] They proposed that faith communities might be fertile ground for health promotion, noting that the support of faith communities in times of family transition could be significant. Petersen has contributed some work on breaking the cycle of school violence but this is from a largely experiential and anecdotal perspective, rather than an evidence-based approach.[40] Rouse described a community-based pediatric clinical experience of parish nursing.[41]

## Social and Geographical Influences on Practice

Tuck and Wallace looked at parish nursing from a hospital-based program in a south-eastern US city.[42] They conducted an exploratory study from two sites. One was an African-American church with a lower income level, and the other a largely white professional congregation with a much higher income level. Both were served by the same hospital system, the nurses being contracted to the churches through the community hospital. They used an ethnographic method to analyze interviews from administrators, spiritual leaders, parish nurses and clients, then a domain analysis and taxonomy for five of the domains. Other than the demographic variations, the health issues consistent with each group, and the differences in worship experience, they (rather surprisingly) found no difference between the two sites. This may have been due to the influence of the accountability and funding structure of the hospital program. Perhaps more research is needed on how

39. Buijs and Olson, "Parish Nursing," 13–23.
40. Peterson, "Breaking the Cycle," 20–23.
41. Rouse, "Parish Nursing," 8–11.
42. Tuck and Wallace, "Exploring Parish Nursing," 290–99.

the age, gender, and ethnic profile of the parish nurse makes a difference to the care that is offered.

Chase-Ziolek and Striepe found some significant differences between urban and rural parish nurse practice in Chicago and Iowa.[43] They compared the type of services provided by volunteer parish nurses in those areas. Notably, that in urban churches 75 percent of contacts that nurses had with individuals took place at the church, whereas in rural settings, only 35 percent of contacts were at the church; the rest were at other locations, home visits or in phone conversations. In the same study they noted the differences in practice offered by volunteer parish nurses from different age groups and ethnic backgrounds.

## Client Response

Wallace, Tuck, Boland and Witacki offered a study concerning the perception of parish nursing from the client's perspective.[44] They used an ethnographic tool to analyze seventeen interviews of clients from two very different American churches, both of which had employed a parish nurse for the preceding four years. Five themes were identified in the responses:

- Availability and approachability;
- Integration of spirituality and health;
- Helping us to help ourselves;
- Exploring parish nursing;
- Evaluating parish nursing.

They found that clients perceived parish nursing as positive and beneficial for the individual, the congregation and the community.

Rethemeyer and Wehling attempted to evaluate the effectiveness of parish nursing in the St. Louis area. Seven hundred and sixty clients served by seventeen parish nurses in five denominations completed a survey using closed ended questions with rating scales. In addition several optional open-ended questions were offered.[45] The results showed that those participating in the survey felt that the congregation benefited from the services offered by the parish nurse. Participants had no problems contacting the

43. Chase-Ziolek and Striepe, "Comparison," 270–79.

44. Wallace et al., "Client Perceptions," 128–35.

45. Rethemeyer and Wehling, "How Are We Doing," 10–12.

nurse, received answers to their questions, and were comfortable praying with the parish nurse. They indicated that she/he encouraged self-development and self-reflection and had a positive impact on their health. The most frequent health practices that were impacted by the parish nurse included; having blood pressure checked regularly (49 percent); participating in worship (41 percent); eating healthier foods (39 percent); learning of the warning signs of a heart attack (39 percent) or stroke (35 percent); attending programs sponsored by the church (35 percent); and getting regular exercise (32 percent).

## The State of Research

Much of the research around spiritual care in American parish nursing lacks specificity in terminology. Burkhart, Konicek, Moorhead, and Androwich, have studied the language used by parish nurses for describing interventions and developed a mapping process to enable the terminology used by parish nurses to be incorporated in the Nursing Interventions Classification system (NIC).[46] This will help to standardize the description of diagnoses and intervention so that data may be more accurately recorded and compared. Such taxonomy will suffice for US parish nursing but UK nursing documentation does not use the US system.

Dyess, Chase, and Newlyn reported the state of research in parish nursing/faith community nursing in 2009 and categorized it in four main content areas: development and implementation of practice; roles and activities of faith community nurses; evaluation and documentation; and congregational experience of faith community nursing.[47] They noted the strength and consistency of publications that report the role and activities of the faith community nurse, but suggest further work is done on

1. The practice linked to a theoretical framework,

2. The role of faith, religion or spirituality within the practice, and

3. The impact on individual and community health outcomes.[48]

46. Burkhart et al., "Mapping Parish Nurse Documentation," 220–29.

47. Dyess et al., "State of Research," 188–99.

48. The terms "parish nursing" and "faith community nursing" are used interchangeably in much of the literature. They refer to the same practice, but parish nursing is always Christian-based whereas faith community nursing may also be based from other faiths.

They suggest all three of these may be due to the fact that many of the nurses are not prepared in research methods. There appears to be an inadequacy of research related to outcomes. There is also a need for further specific research on the role of faith in parish nursing. Much of the research and education for parish nursing in the US is rooted in the discipline of nursing rather than the discipline of theological study and this may be a reason for the paucity of evidence on the relationship between faith and spiritual care in parish nursing.

## THE UNIQUENESS OF PARISH NURSING IN A UK CHURCH CONTEXT

As previously noted with reference to the deaconess movement, the role of nurses working from churches in the later part of the nineteenth century and early twentieth century was quite common in the UK. Clergy were sometimes involved in the commencement and/or management of voluntary hospitals.[49] As these hospitals moved to NHS management the role of the clergy in them was confined to pastoral care through the chaplaincy chaplaincy department.

In contemporary church life in the UK, the larger churches employ a variety of staff and appoint a range of volunteers. Alongside the priest, the minister, or the person who holds pastoral charge, there are assistant or associate ministers, youth ministers, and evangelists. Most of the above will have had formal theological training and many will have held posts in other occupations before entering church ministry. Some will have professional experience in the health services, and they will draw on this professional knowledge as they serve the church and its community. In addition, churches now employ detached youth workers and family workers; and they appoint pastoral care leaders along with pastoral care volunteers. As has been seen, parish nurses do not do injections, dressings, or invasive treatments. So how is the work of a parish nurse unique? How might it differ from, say, the work of a children and families specialist?

The difference between these ministries and a parish nurse ministry is that the latter is focused specifically in the area of health. The definition of health is broad, but the expression of a parish nurse ministry will be limited by the competences for which the nurse has been trained. People both inside and outside of the church's influence recognize that they have health

49. Stout, *History of North Ormesby Hospital*, 12.

needs, and so the nurse can build a bridge of communication by offering care and concern at that point of need. Health knowledge is named and put into practice, and the nurse remains registered with the Nursing and Midwifery Council. She/he therefore works within the code of practice that is laid down by that professional body.[50] She/he is bound to keep records and to observe the rules of confidentiality. This is a deeply significant issue for churches, where records are not usually kept, let alone in locked cabinets, and where confidentiality around personal issues is often difficult to maintain. For the parish nurse, the health needs of the client and respect for their dignity and choice are paramount. She/he has to keep up to date with evidence-based health information, and work in cooperation with other members of the healthcare team. That brings both a need to develop good relationships with General Practitioners and other health care providers. As a fellow-professional in health, she/he understands the language and shares common qualifications with nurses who work in those organizations.

Many churches seek the good of the community in which they are placed. They already offer interventions in mental and spiritual health through pastoral care programs and activities for those that attend worship, or linked activities. The parish nurse is in a unique position to engage with physical health needs in this and in the wider community while at the same time giving help around spiritual, mental, and community health needs. Furthermore, she/he may provide knowledge of disease management and contemporary treatments that will help the pastoral care team to care for those with medical needs more effectively. For all these activities she/he will train and coordinate volunteers as co-workers, thus facilitating the involvement of both members of the congregation and clients in the service of others.

Family workers and youth leaders also recruit volunteers but focus on the needs of the younger age group. Elder care workers focus on third and fourth agers.[51] Social workers deal mainly with people from disadvantaged backgrounds. The parish nurse, however, may work with people of all ages and all backgrounds.

50. "Code of Practice."

51. Third agers are active older people, who may or may not be recently retired. Fourth agers are less active, usually in their eighties or nineties.

## THE UNIQUENESS OF PARISH NURSING
## IN A UK HEALTH CARE CONTEXT

In the early nineteenth century, men who professed to have medical and surgical skills abounded, but their numbers decreased as they began to be registered and the process of professionalization began. Nurses at that time were likened to servants. They did very menial tasks, including the cleaning and scrubbing of ward floors, and were often drawn from the uneducated classes. The matrons, though, sometimes came from more middle-class backgrounds. Community health care came in the form of largely untrained "handywomen," who fulfilled "a traditional social and economic role in the local community, remaining serious competitors to certified midwives and district nurses until the 1930s and 1940s."[52] In the workhouses other inmates provided most of the direct care.[53] As Nightingale reformed the image of nursing, things began to change, especially from a nurse leadership perspective.

> A prominent input of religious ideals and social conscience, Matron inspired inspired Christian values and respectability. A religious background was viewed as essential in coping with suffering and death and as a means of consoling patients.[54]

The medical profession, by this time well-established, participated in the three-year training of nurses, which initiated the process of professionalization. Until the 1970s, training was integrated with work on the wards and was totally based in hospitals. Universities then began to deliver nurse education. Midwifery developed a parallel road. Health visiting started in 1862 through the Manchester and Salford Ladies Sanitary Reform Association. These "sanitary inspectors" had a role in promoting hygiene, but would often also tend the sick as they found them. In the early twentieth century, health visitors often had a background training in nursing, but this was not mandatory until 1965.[55] District nursing grew from the Ranyard nurses, who had a religious foundation. From these roots grew the contemporary range of registered nurses that are found in the NHS today: hospital based nurses and midwives with various specialisms, nurse educators, mental

---

52. Dingwall et al., "Nurses and Servants," 127–28.

53. Ibid., 128.

54. Lorentzon and Bryant "Leadership," 272.

55. "A Health Visiting Timeline."

health nurses, community nurses and midwives, nurse practitioners, health visitors, school nurses, practice nurses, and occupational health nurses.

Unlike the days before Nightingale reformed the image of nursing, contemporary nurses are often viewed with a degree of trust. People ask intimate questions of nurses that they would not even necessarily ask of a doctor, let alone a member of the clergy. One general practitioner has noted that patients will allow nurses to touch them in appropriate ways that signify care when words are not enough, which he deems to be more difficult for non-nursing professionals.[56] Nurses are usually welcomed and valued in the home when needs arise. NHS care is augmented by private agency nurses, and charity-based nursing: Macmillan and Marie Curie nurses provide specialized care for cancer patients. Admiral Nurses now provide extra care for dementia sufferers. So how is parish nursing unique in the public sphere today?

Parish nurse caseloads are not defined by the type of condition in which they specialize, or by the social background of the client. They will visit anyone with any health need. Unlike NHS nurses, they are not bound by given amounts of time per patient; they manage their own practice and take as many or as few clients as their time allows. When they work with a client, they have in their bag of resources a number of additional support interventions that can be offered from volunteers linked to the local churches. These can be in the form of pastoral care, practical help with shopping, cleaning and cooking, reading, music, transport, outings, care relief, interest groups, or just good company. They can refer people to other voluntary providers, or to activities that currently happen at local churches. This gives anyone with a health need access to a wide range of community support possibilities. It gives the client choice of access to someone who will come with the recommendation of a local church, and will include spiritual care as part of their remit without any pressure to change religion or join a particular group. If the client is a Christian believer, a parish nurse will understand some of the spiritual needs that might be affecting their sense of well being. For anyone seeking answers to theological questions, the parish nurse may be their means of access to an appropriate religious leader.

For those who need a sense of purpose, and the opportunity to give something back to society, the parish nurse may also be the key to their

56. Dr Malcom Rigler who first invited Ann Solari-Twadell to the UK to speak about parish nursing, often quotes this when recommending parish nursing to groups of interested professionals.

involvement in volunteering, helping others toward health, which in turn will bring a sense of dignity and well-being.

When a hospital nurse is faced with someone who needs spiritual care alongside physical or mental health care, hospital chaplains may be called. But when that person goes home, the hospital based chaplaincy service is not usually available and there are very few NHS community health chaplains. The presence of a parish nurse in a locality offers the chaplaincy service a way of addressing this problem and strengthening their links with local churches. With the patient's permission they can make a referral in the knowledge that the parish nurse is working to national standards of practice in confidentiality and teamwork. She/he will also be able to understand and monitor the patient's physical condition, perhaps preventing them from complications and an unnecessary health crisis, and thus reducing the likelihood of a subsequent emergency return to hospital.

NHS community nurses and health visitors are hard pressed to cover all the needs of patients, especially in the face of cutbacks and an ageing population with ever greater health challenges. Parish nurses are uniquely placed to enhance the work of the community health services, promoting their healthy living message and looking out for the vulnerable. They have the potential to reach those who because of work pressures, career responsibilities, dis-like of medical visits, cultural or language barriers, or fear of state-linked intervention, do not seek health advice when they need it.

## SPIRITUALITY AND RELIGION
## IN THE UK HEALTH CARE CONTEXT

The various definitions of spirituality referred to in chapter one show a broad range of views around the concept. This was illustrated at a UK conference on spirituality in nursing in 2009.[57] Speakers included Revd. Professor Stephen Wright MBE, who presented a paper evidencing a connection between spirituality and wellbeing; John Paley, Senior lecturer in Nursing and Midwifery at the University of Stirling who, following his series of articles on the subject, suggested that the terms spirituality and spiritual care could be so ill-defined as to be meaningless; and Dr Suman

57. In April 2009, the publishing company of the Royal College of Nursing held a study day entitled "The Spirit of Nursing," in which a variety of speakers were invited to participate from different perspectives. This event included a seminar on Parish nursing. Abstracts were subsequently published on the website of the Nursing Standard.

Fernando, who contributed a perspective on mental health and spirituality. Each of these defined spirituality in a slightly different way. They were followed by Revd Tom Keighley who described the historical relationship between faith traditions and nursing.

McSherry has shown that nursing has indeed had a strong historical link with religious and spiritual traditions.[58] This was seen in Europe and the UK, in an era where churchgoing was much more common, and was especially expressed through the established churches. Some parts of the contemporary welfare state came about as a result of the religious philanthropists. But the scene in contemporary Britain has changed. People sometimes describe themselves as not religious, but spiritual. Chryssides and Geaves write of a line now being drawn between religion and spirituality; they suggest that

> The traditional churches are associated with religion and a lack of spirituality, and perceived to be dull, conformist and doctrinally rigid . . . Religion, then, is perceived to be not the repository of spirituality, but even the antithesis of the spiritual.[59]

Berger, Davie, and Fokas contrast Europe with America in this respect.[60] They see Western and Northern Europe as an exception to the rest of the world when it comes to the place of religion in society. Even within Europe, they identify difference. Whereas France is very clearly secular, religious institutions in Italy and Finland play a greater part in society. They note that in Europe, religion is sometimes seen as part of the problem, whereas in America and other countries it is seen as part of the solution. So in the US, where the church has, ironically, always been separated from the state, the religious aspects of spiritual care are more pronounced. Hence the relative normality in the US of providing social care services from the churches. John Paley, however, regards America as the exceptional case, with Europe and the UK now seen as "secular." In light of this he promotes a helpful discussion of the extent to which a Christian understanding of spirituality has relevance in a secular environment.[61] The clear implication from this is that parish nurses working from churches in a less religious society need to find rigorous ways of ensuring that vulnerable clients have

58. McSherry, *Spirituality in Nursing*, 17–36

59. Chryssides and Geaves, *Study of Religion*, 198–99.

60. Berger et al, *Religious America*, 44–45

61. Paley, "Religion and Secularisation," 1963–74.

choices at all times and that respect is given to those that would prefer not to discuss religion or receive prayer.

Many of the contributions on parish nursing from academics and practitioners hail from North America, where the health services are often attached to religious institutions. In the UK, since the advent of the state-funded National Health Service, this is no longer the case.[62] Yet in 1970, the ward sister on a medical ward at St Bartholomew's hospital in London would ring a small bell for silence and then lead daily morning and evening (Christian) prayers. In her absence the staff nurse would repeat the process, whether or not she/he was a believer. This practice gradually ceased in UK hospitals depending on the attitude of the staff involved, or the governing board of the hospital. It followed the pattern of gradual decline in church attendance which will be referred to in chapter 3 of this book. The NHS does still fund multi-faith chaplaincy services, largely based in hospitals, to address the holistic and individualized needs of patients. In some places these have been under threat from management teams in a money-saving approach. Castledine notes with concern their view of the work of the chaplain as "based on religious dogma, its value being difficult to evaluate."[63]

The NHS has produced guidelines on respecting the beliefs and religious practices of both patients and staff.[64] The minimum religious requirements and procedures for the particular faith community to which the patient owns allegiance, are therefore usually respected, with perhaps an occasional visit from one of the volunteers with the Health Care chaplaincy team. It could therefore be argued that at least in hospitals, such religious needs are being met where they are stated, or requested by patients, especially in relation to ritual and sacrament. There is also some recognition that spiritual care is important, though as has been seen, what is meant by the term and how this is delivered varies enormously.

If the concept of spiritual care includes attention to the search for meaning and purpose in life, the relationship between mind and body, the ability to use freedom of choice, and the connection with oneself and others and in relationship to a higher power, and if it is seen as having relevance to health, then there is an area of overlap with what is available in the Christian gospel, and also with what is offered in other faiths.

62. There is only one specifically Christian hospital in England, Burrswood, near Tunbridge Wells in Kent, which is privately operated as a charity.

63. Castledine, "Spiritual State," 803.

64. Department of Health, "Religion or Belief."

There are a number of studies showing that some physical or mental health problems can be alleviated by religious practices or faith development, and that some conditions are less prevalent in certain faith communities. Plante and Sherman, again from an American context, review the literature supporting three aspects of this link:

1. That some religious communities are less susceptible to certain conditions due to their rules of behavior (e.g. less incidence of AIDS transmission in communities where sexual practice is confined to marriage);

2. That religiousness and spirituality affect how an individual adapts or copes with an illness once diagnosed; and

3. More controversially, how the presence of active faith may have influence on physiological or mental processes.[65]

None of this proves that faith affects health in an objective way; it does however suggest the act of believing and/or attending religious worship makes a difference.

If there is a minimalist approach to religion and spirituality in the UK health context, or a failure to recognize the overlap between these two concepts and their relationship to physical or mental health, does that matter? Could this lead to a paucity of understanding about the ways in which health problems may be influenced by spiritual need? Notwithstanding the answer to that, such an approach does seem to reduce the thinking of congregations and health care delivery organizations to a dualist perspective on health, which limits the ways in which faith communities may contribute to the delivery of whole-person care. At a time when the health service has undergone another re-structuring, when the focus of health care is moving towards the community rather than hospital, and when the government is looking for participation from the voluntary sector, the involvement of faith groups could be useful, even if only to assist the health promotion agenda. This could be of even greater relevance in the minority ethnic communities, where religious adherence is generally higher and health services are not always so often utilized.

65. Plante and Sherman, *Faith and Health*, 3–5.

## PARISH NURSING RESEARCH IN THE UK

Being a relatively new movement in the UK, specific UK research on parish nursing is in its infancy. There have been three further pieces of work so far completed in addition to my original dissertation.[66] In 2005 a study was made of the tasks that parish nurses most often do in the UK as a comparison with parish nurses in America and Swaziland. It was led by Professor Ann Solari-Twadell, conducted by the Revd. Nigel Ford, and reported upon at the Westberg Symposium in 2007. Twelve UK nurses participated, but they were in a very early stage of their practice. The methodology used had been developed in the US and designed with different terminology for a much larger sample of parish nurse participation, so its suitability for assessing UK practice was therefore limited. It did however show that the most frequent interventions used in the UK were active listening and exercise promotion. This was similar to the US results, but very different to those from the Swaziland sample, which demonstrated a stronger emphasis on practical nursing care in homes.[67]

The other two studies are BA and MA dissertations respectively: Kim Wilson has completed a survey on the way in which faith contributes to coping with chronic illness;[68] and Jennie Fytche a thesis on the spirituality of children, from the perspective of a parish nurse.[69] Two further studies are soon to be available: one on crisis intervention, and another on helping people prepare well for their own death.

## ENGLISH CHURCHES AND PARISH NURSING

Castledine comments that some of those who study the areas of overlap between spiritual care or religious observance and mental/physical health care in the UK do seem to invite more practitioners into this field, although he also notes that there are major economic issues to be faced if churches are to take part in parish nursing.[70] Many English churches have at least one registered nurse in their congregation. Most have someone who has at one time been a registered nurse. Even if a nurse volunteers to take on the

66. Wordsworth, "Parish Nursing."
67. Solari-Twadell et al., "What do Parish Nurses Do?"
68. Fytche, "Parish Nursing."
69. Wilson, "Christian Faith."
70. Castledine, "Spiritual State," 803.

role without remuneration, there are expenses to be refunded and fees for professional training and support to be paid. A back-to-nursing course will need to be undertaken by those whose registration has lapsed. At a time of financial restraint, nurses may not be able to take a reduction in income, and churches will need to decide whether or not to offer paid hours. In making such a decision they will need to assess the extent to which the range of interventions that could be offered by a parish nurse is likely to contribute to their mission strategy. That demands a comprehensive understanding of the nature of their mission task.

## SUMMARY

Parish nursing seeks to improve and add value to the coordination of healthcare around an individual or a community, through a congregation. The (mostly American) research on practice shows that it clearly has the potential to do this, although more work on outcomes and theological foundations are necessary. If a church sees the improvement of physical health care as part of its mission then the literature suggests that the appointment of a parish nurse could further this aim. Definitions of spiritual care and spirituality are broad and difficult to specify. If they include a person's understanding of meaning and purpose to life, or connection with a higher being, then discussions around those issues might also relate to the mission of a local church. Much depends on how the local church understands its mission and this will be explored in the next chapter.

# 3

# Towards an Understanding of the Mission of an English Church

In America, hospitals are largely commercial entities, many of which are attached to religious denominations and have links with local churches. Some parish nurses are employed by these hospitals. Others are employed by a denomination or regional network. If they are appointed by local churches, they usually have much larger congregations than in the UK; much of the work of an American parish nurse is directed at the members of the congregation rather than members of the public that do not attend church at all.[1] In the UK, hospitals are largely owned and funded by the government. Unlike their American counterparts, UK parish nurses are never employed or coordinated by or through hospital systems. Neither are they employed or appointed nationally or regionally by any denomination. Rather, they are attached to a local church, or a specific local expression of a denominational or national network of churches. Their congregations are likely to be small in comparison and there is a greater focus on outreach work. In such a context the potential of parish nursing for enhancement of the mission of an English church should exist. The research question asked how far parish nursing actually does make a difference to the mission of an English church. In order to answer that question, it was necessary first to

1. In other countries, such as New Zealand and Canada, parish nurses are more often found to be working with people outside of the church. This may reflect a more similar ecclesiological and healthcare context to the UK.

clarify what is meant by an "English church" and explore the nature of and rationale behind an English church's mission.[2]

For the purposes of this research the definition of an English church has been understood as being a local expression of Christian church geographically placed in England. Most UK parish nurses work with Anglican or Baptist congregations, but they may be found in many denominations and they work with churches of all sizes. That local expression of church could therefore be from any Christian tradition with a "membership" of under ten to over two hundred. It could be rural, suburban, urban, urban housing estate, or situated in a hybrid of any of these. Although Catholic churches have parish nurses in other parts of the world, as yet there are not many Roman Catholic churches in England that have appointed a parish nurse, and so this research project was necessarily limited in that it only examined the concept of parish nursing in a Protestant context.[3]

Many factors will affect a local church's attitude to its mission. These include the context in which the church is placed; the cultural perspectives and abilities of its members; the age, availability, and work patterns of its congregation; the encouragement or otherwise of its leadership; its theological position; the passion and educational training of its preachers; its ecclesiology; its missiological understanding; and the historical and pragmatic factors that have influenced it. This chapter will explore some of these factors, in order to come to some understanding of how churches have come to perceive their mission; it will look more specifically at three theological themes that seem to be particularly relevant to the ministry of parish nursing; and from these discussions it will seek to identify a set of criteria against which an examination of the impact of parish nursing upon a church's mission may be conducted.

## HISTORICAL AND PRAGMATIC INFLUENCES

Both the amount of volunteer work with which a church can engage, and the extent of its paid mission work, depend on the number of people who

2. There are parish nurses in Scotland and Wales too but the studies herein described were limited to English locations.

3. This is in part due to the slow but steady growth of parish nursing in the UK with its limited finance and staffing capabilities and the subsequent limitations of promotional activity into all denominations. At the time of writing, the first Catholic parish nursing project is underway and it is hoped there will be more to come.

identify with that church, and the amount of time or money they can contribute.

Churchgoing statistics vary according to the way in which questions are asked, the samples of whom they are asked, and the truthfulness of the replies.[4] In America, the commonly quoted statistic for those who say they are churchgoers is 40 percent of the population, and in 2005 Gallup found it to be 41 percent.[5] But in the UK churchgoing is now a less popular activity. The earliest records derive from an ecclesiastical census in 1851, which revealed that 59 percent of the English population attended church.[6] However, this figure does not exclude children or those making multiple visits to church on the one Sunday that it was recorded—March 30, 1851. An estimate given by one scholar is that nearer 40 percent of the English adult population attended church at least once on that Sunday.[7]

Church going began to decline after the 1880s, and more rapidly after 1920 except for some rallying in the 1950s. There are many reasons suggested for the decline, including the effect of enlightenment thinking, the suffering of two world wars, and controversially, the change in cultural and work-life behavior brought about by the changing role of women.[8] Estimates by Christian Research, considered by scholars to be consistent in method if not totally accurate,[9] suggested that just 9.9 percent of the English population attended church on one Sunday in 1989 reducing to 6.3 percent in 2005. And yet in the census of 2001, 72 percent of the population of England declared their religion to be Christian and in 2011 the figure declined further to 59 percent.[10] Even though the trend is downwards, and even though churchgoing has declined, the majority of the population still prefer to be categorized as Christian. This is sometimes called popular religion, or "believing without belonging."[11] But in a study of one North Yorkshire village, Steve Bruce examined the decline of church-going and states

4. For a discussion of the accuracy of church attendance figures in both the US and the UK see Hadaway and Marler, "Did You Really Go To Church?"

5. Gallup, "Church Attendance USA."

6. Brown, *Death of Christian Britain*, 161.

7. Ibid., 162.

8. Ibid., 169. Brown's rather controversial thesis is that much of this change is related to the role of women in society. But see also Bruce, "Demise of Christianity," 54; Gilbert, "Secularization and the Future," 512.

9. Brierley, *Pulling out of the Nosedive*, 12.

10. H.M. Government, "National Statistics 2001, and 2011."

11. Davie, *Religion in Britain*, 45.

that this "popular religion is doubly vulnerable."[12] He suggests that it is not only affected by the sociological changes that affect churches, but that as churches cease to exist, so the very opportunities for maintaining a Christian identity, such as baptism, marriage, funerals, and attendance at Sunday school, Christmas and Easter are reduced. The implication for churches from this argument is that reducing the availability of institutional church life in a community speeds the decline of popular religion.

Clearly, the number of people available to be involved in mission from the churches is now significantly lower than it was in the middle of the twentieth century, although it cannot be assumed that all those who attended church in the 1950s would have been engaged in missional activities.

Numbers and resources have not been the only factors affecting the church's mission in the last century, nor can they form a measurement of effectiveness. Inspired by the nineteenth century reformers, some of whom were impelled by their faith, many early twentieth century Christians were deeply involved in serving the poor, the sick, and the orphan. Whilst the context of Christendom, in which these acts of service were made, was not necessarily the rationale for these works of charity, it did provide a context in which faith-sharing could be naturally incorporated.[13] Mission projects abroad multiplied as travel became more possible, and these involved medical care in an integrated way with education and preaching of the gospel. The religious elements in the emergence of nursing institutions in Victorian times are sometimes forgotten but clearly present in the historical records.[14] "Bible nurses" did home visiting in London's slum areas, armed with various health remedies and a Bible.[15] Before the introduction of the NHS in 1948, the church's mission in England was much more wholistic than it is today. But as the government began to take on responsibilities for health and relief of poverty, so the involvement of faith groups in these activities began to diminish. Although freedom to hold Christian acts of worship in state-run healthcare facilities remained, the trend was to minimize these so that by 1980, as we have seen, the practice of the ward sister reading morning and evening prayers on a daily basis had all but ceased. Patients who required any form of Christian spiritual care whilst in hospital were referred to the chaplain, and any services of worship that were

12. Bruce, "Secularisation," 544.

13. Powell, "West Ham Philanthropic Institutions."

14. Prochaska, *Christianity and Social Service,* 123–27.

15. Ibid. These were later to become Ranyard nurses.

organized were safely tucked away out of sight in hospital chapels. Statutory provision was beginning to exclude faith-based activities in the NHS for all but those who sought them out, and slowly, imperceptibly perhaps, this tendency became normative. The mission of the local church in England was now perceived by many outside the church as being mostly about spiritual issues, rather than those relating to the promotion of physical health. The notable contrast to this was where church members became missionaries abroad; in that context, the wholistic nature of the mission continued.

Another factor was at work in the English churches. Between 1950 and 1986 the preaching tours of evangelists like Billy Graham and Luis Palau brought new converts into the churches, but the emphasis of these evangelists was upon the case for spiritual conversion rather than the physical aspects of the gospel. The rise of the charismatic movement in the sixties and seventies re-focused some minds on physical health but on the miraculous aspects of healing rather than healthy living advice. Others turned away from any focus on healing. The gap between physical health and spiritual health grew more obvious. It was at this time that Scorer made a case for churches to keep out of the health scene altogether.[16]

The distance between the spiritual and physical health implications of the corporate English church's action in mission had therefore widened, although the concern by individual Christians to participate in the care of civic society remained, for example in areas like drug rehabilitation.[17] This is illustrated in the example of Bromley-by-Bow, where a healthy living centre developed in the church building alongside a GP surgery. Many excellent community services were provided, inspired by a Christian GP's personal faith and understanding of mission, but there was no specific integration with a verbal expression of the gospel, and there is now no link with the church. Some churches, for example, Halcon Baptist Church in Taunton, linked up with the local health service to provide NHS clinics in their building but crucially, apart from the provision of rented space, there was no specific faith input to these activities.

The nineties saw the outworking of a decade of word-based evangelism, with four notable elements: the church growth movement, that had peaked in the 1980s, was still influential; large, seeker-sensitive churches like Willow Creek and Saddleback grew strongly; a church planting movement

16. Scorer, "Healing."

17. Yeldall Manor, a drug rehabilitation center, was begun in the 1970s by a Youth For Christ evangelist.

was energized by the D.A.W.N. congress in 1992; and a charismatic phenomenon called the "Toronto Blessing" crossed international boundaries. Most of these influences did not specifically focus on charitable works in their initial stages, although they did begin to develop some social projects as well. The Christian initiation course "Alpha" spread widely across many denominations. While this, along with similar courses, has remained an important means of explaining the gospel, it has not been associated with a large-scale commitment to social action.[18]

The dichotomy between spiritual and physical interventions by the local church persisted. It was fuelled by the secularization of state health provision, and the reluctance of grant-making bodies to offer churches money for social projects. So in England in the early 1990s, wholistic ideals held by individual Christians were usually enacted through their personal involvement in independent charities or the state sector.

In the last fifteen years there has however been a discernible swing back to significant social concern by evangelical churches. Two movements have led the way: "TEAR fund," founded in 1968 for international wholistic relief work began working with "Livability," (formerly the Shaftesbury society and the John Grooms Association), to help UK churches engage with issues of poverty. And "Oasis/Faithworks," whose initial activities in youth work and church planting training, have gradually developed into more of a social action focus. Each of these has produced training packs for church members and lists of ways in which churches may participate in community development. Faithworks has produced a charter for social action that helps churches to convince local government funders of their trustworthiness.[19] They have networks throughout the UK that focus on encouraging churches in social action and community development. The "Church Urban Fund," and the Catholic social action umbrella, "Caritas," have similar resources available to all churches. Rural churches may find social action resources at the Arthur Rank Centre in Stoneleigh, Warwickshire.

18. A sister organization, "Besom," grew out of "Alpha" in the 1980s as a means of helping the poor, but in comparison had very little publicity. In 2011 it had just 30 branches in the UK. Holy Trinity Brompton, "Besom: Sweep Away Suffering."

19. "The Faithworks Charter."

## MISSIOLOGICAL UNDERSTANDING

In order to participate more fully in wholistic mission, a church needs to understand why it is doing so. Some churches will see mission primarily as evangelism, others as overseas work, as church-planting, social action, community development, creation care, or prophetic declaration. Some will set aside specific individuals for the purpose, others will view mission as the responsibility of all.

Mission can be seen as "both the mother of theology and of the church."[20] In this perspective the local church is therefore the mission agency as a whole, rather than a community that identifies one or two individuals who believe they have a calling and sends them off somewhere. A helpful way of perceiving the relationship between ecclesiology and missiology comes from Craig Van Gelder: "The church is mission, the church does what it is, the church organizes what it does."[21] Yet those who see their religion as more of a private affair may not be inclined towards this concept at all. So what has contributed to a congregation's perception of its mission?

Mission thinking has been inspired throughout the twentieth century by a series of conferences, emanating from Edinburgh 1910, when protestant mission organizations from across the world met together to consider the task of global mission. Attendance was usually limited to delegates, and some have suggested that their influence on their return to local churches was minimal.[22] But the work achieved at these meetings was gradually filtered through mission agencies and theological colleges. Some of these conferences were particularly noted for specific outcomes: Edinburgh (1910) for its ecumenical approach to mission—the coming together of different Christian denominations to consider mission strategy. This is currently mirrored in the interdenominational training and resourcing of parish nursing both worldwide and nationally. Brandenburg (1932) was noted for Karl Barth's thinking about mission as the activity of God himself, and Willingen (1952) for its focus on God's ownership of mission and use of the phrase *Missio Dei*.[23] These meetings gave emphasis to the work of God in the world, and this is the influence behind the perception

---

20. Stevens, *Abolition of the Laity*, 197.

21. Van Gelder, *Ministry of the Missional Church*, 17.

22. The impact of these conferences is assessed by Gunther, "History and Significance," 521–37.

23. Stevens, *Abolition of the Laity*, 193.

of parish nursing as a missional activity, as well as a means of pastoral care for church members.

The Lausanne movement was initiated by a conference of evangelicals in 1974.[24] A covenant was drawn up that focused largely on evangelism in relation to the spiritual condition. There was no reference to health or healing. Social action was seen as a separate activity, but at least a duty of the Christian. To some extent this helped in the orientation of evangelicals towards a concern for physical needs, notably justice, reconciliation, and the dignity of all people, at least in theory if not in practice.

This was strengthened in the follow-up to the first Lausanne conference, held in Manila in 1989. The title was "Proclaim Christ until He Comes: Calling the Whole Church to Take the Whole Gospel to the Whole World."[25] It had a manifesto that included statements on Christ as the only way to God: the call to care for those deprived of justice, dignity, food, and shelter; the need for every member of the church to be involved in mission; the affirming of gifting and partnership of women and men in evangelization; the requirement for every Christian congregation to turn itself outward to its local community in witness and service; and the commitment that every church should study the society in which it lives, in order to develop appropriate strategies for mission.[26] This time, the words "minister to the sick, feed the hungry" were included. Further, in contrast to the Lausanne covenant of 1974, good news and good works were said to be inseparable. A critique of the Manila manifesto was that it offered a rather paternalistic focus on the poor as unreached peoples, not as equal partners.[27] But at least it gave evangelical churches a much stronger foundation for compassionate service, and opened the way for initiatives like parish nursing to be included in their mission strategies. It also encouraged the involvement of every member in mission. This corresponds to the encouragement of volunteering by church members, which is part of a parish nurse job description.

The third Lausanne Conference took place in Cape Town in 2010 with the intention of looking at poverty in more depth. The first part of the official report of its work includes a section on love for the world's poor

24. The movement actually began with regional conferences like the European Congress on Evangelism in Amsterdam in 1971.

25. Lausanne, "Gatherings, Lausanne ii."

26. Lausanne, "Manila Manifesto."

27. Steuernagel, "Social Concern," 53–56.

and suffering, including the promotion of justice, and part two calls people to action on slavery and human trafficking, and poverty. It suggests that churches should go beyond providing medical and social care for people who have disabilities, towards inclusion and the enabling of their gifts in service to others.[28] The influence of this gathering is yet to be seen, but if it follows previous conferences it will filter through to local congregations via theological colleges and ministers. The implication for parish nursing is that in addition to offering compassionate service, churches need to find ways of enabling service users to become service deliverers; they need to include those who receive care among their teams of volunteers.

Within the Roman Catholic Church, such statements have greater authority, since they come from the Pope. Vatican II, pronounced after three years of consultation in 1965, produced two decrees of particular relevance to Catholics, but they were also welcomed by those in the wider church. One concerned the encouragement of Catholics to engage in ecumenical activities, and another commended mission as the task of all Catholics. This was defined as that activity which makes Christ and therefore the church (members) fully present to all men or nations. Where it is not possible to speak of the faith, the mission must be maintained by "charity and by works of mercy, with all patience, prudence and great confidence."[29]

The Anglican Consultative Council developed the following guidelines, "The Five Marks of Mission," between 1984 and 1990.[30]

The mission of the Church is the mission of Christ

1. To proclaim the Good News of the Kingdom;

2. To teach baptize and nurture new believers;

3. To respond to human need by loving service;

4. To seek to transform unjust structures of society;

5. To strive to safeguard the integrity of creation and sustain and renew the life of the earth.

Marks three, four, and five are of particular relevance to the ministry of parish nursing. Discussions have since developed around these guidelines

---

28. Lausanne, "Cape Town Commitment."

29. Christus Rex, "Vatican II on Mission."

30. Church of England, "Five Marks of Mission."

and there is a move to include liturgy as mission and to encourage congregations to "be" a people of mission as well as to do it.[31]

"Mission-shaped church" was largely concerned with church planting. Published in 2004 by the Church of England's mission and public affairs council, it added five values of a missionary church to the five marks of mission. Notably these did not include responding to human need or safeguarding creation, and said little about transforming society.[32] Examples of "fresh expressions" of church were given and congregations urged to develop more of these. The "Fresh Expressions" movement has since grown to include Methodist work and offers training courses and resources. It continues to grow and to influence thinking about the mission of local churches. A few of the stories on the website refer to social action beyond evangelism, but most focus on a culturally relevant word-based, or fresh liturgical approach.[33]

In 2001 leaders from 140 Christian organizations involved with poverty met in Oxford to discuss social action and evangelism and came up with a statement known as the Micah Declaration.[34] They proposed the use of the phrase, "Integral Mission," by which they meant that not only are evangelism and social action to be done alongside each other in a wholistic manner but that proclamation and demonstration of the gospel are to be implemented in an integrated way. In practice this is more difficult to achieve, at least in the West, largely because of political sensitivity about faith-based initiatives in a secular context. Efforts to address the relationship between faith and social action are needed. The typology of mission orientation offered by Unruh and Sider from their study of fifteen churches in Philadelphia may be helpful:[35]

- dominant social action, where addressing social concerns is the primary mission;

- dual focus, where evangelism and social ministry are independent areas of ministry;

- holistic, where evangelism and social ministry are dynamically interconnected;

31. Ibid., para 4, 5.
32. Church of England, *Mission-Shaped Church*, 31
33. "Who Are We?" *Fresh Expressions*.
34. "Micah Network Declaration." See also Thacker and Hoek, *Micah's Challenge*.
35. Unruh and Sider, *Saving Souls*, 134.

- dominant evangelism, where sharing the gospel is the primary mission;
- inwardly focused, where there is no significant social action or evangelism.[36]

## THE BIBLICAL IMPERATIVE

We have seen that churches plan their mission activity under the influence of history, and by the understandings that come to them through their leaders from various conferences of missiologists. Week by week however they are inspired, or not, by homilies or exposition from preachers who may claim to have Biblical authority for their sermons. They receive this through various translations of the text itself but usually with the help of commentators and missiologists. Some focus on key texts in the New Testament as foundational for mission, seeing it as the beginning of a series of paradigm changes in missional history.[37] For them the Old Testament contributes to these changes purely as an underlying narrative. Where there are instances of missiological engagement, such as the story of the sending of Jonah to Nineveh, the messenger is seen as the prophet of doom rather than the bringer of potential blessing.[38]

An alternative view is that there is some continuity between the Old and New Testaments. *Heilsgeschichte* (salvation-history) links both Testaments in a view of mission that tends towards the verbal, intentional, purposeful proclamation of the gospel message as primary. It would incline away from a very broad definition of mission.[39]

The Old Testament affirms the election of Israel as a God's chosen people. Yet there is a paradox here because they are also given instructions relating to the blessing of other nations. Senior and Stuhlmueller note that the Hebrew verb *Bahar* (he chose) has an integral implication of being chosen for a particular purpose or mission. They note that in the second part of Isaiah's prophecy, where the larger world is included more fully in Israel's perspective of the future, this purpose is expressed more clearly.[40] They go on to identify five features of the ministry of Jesus "that eventually

36. Ibid., 135–48.
37. Bosch, *Transforming Mission*, 15.
38. Jonah 3–1.
39. Köstenberger, "Place of Mission," 347–62.
40. Senior and Stuhlmueller, *Biblical Foundations*, 94.

would nourish the early church's sense of mission": his extraordinary piety evident in his close relationship with God; his compassion to peripheral people, like the poor, the tax-collector, the Samaritan; his interpretation of the law in the light of the love command; his teaching on reconciliation and forgiveness, even extending to enemies and repetitive sins; and his ministry of healings and exorcisms, demonstrating God's concern for human life beyond personal guilt and broken relationships.[41]

From yet another perspective, all mission emanates from a Trinitarian understanding of God. This emphasis was resurrected by Karl Barth and underlies the post-Willingen basis for missional theology in the Western church.[42] "If God the Father sends God the Son into the world to offer the gift of life, and together they send God the Holy Spirit, then the church, which receives that Spirit, receives someone who in very nature, is a sending being."[43] Mission therefore becomes the church's participation in the sending of God.[44] Eastern churches may see this in a different light, because of their different understanding of the genesis of the Holy Spirit.

A more recent and comprehensive study by C. J. H. Wright sees the whole Bible as the product of God's mission.[45] Genesis 12:3, where God sends Abraham to a land yet to be revealed, is seen as a foundational text in mission: "I will bless those who bless you and whoever curses you I will curse; and all peoples on earth will be blessed through you."[46]

If this is the will and purpose of the one trinitarian God, then it is also the goal of the church of Christ, and paints for us a broader canvas of universal mission. It is a picture that includes the concepts of redemption and rescue, justice, inclusivity, restoration and healing, holiness, and even creation care. It compels us to consider the connections between each of these concepts. For example, the new believer's transformed thinking about Jesus' teaching on material gain influences changed lifestyle behavior which is connected with issues of both fair trade and environmental pollution. Action that results from this may bless the lives of people in poorer parts of

---

41. Ibid., 145–49.

42. Simpson, "Reformation," 75.

43. This idea is explored further in Peskett and Ramachandra, *Message of Mission*, 11.

44. Bosch, *Transforming Mission*, 390.

45. Wright, *Mission of God*, 51.

46. Gen 12:3.

the world. Seen in this light, there is little biblical evidence to distinguish a narrow definition of mission.

But "if everything is mission then nothing is mission."[47] This often-quoted phrase is sometimes used as a caution against a broad definition of mission. It may also be a response to a mistaken assumption about the need for action in mission. In the 1950s and 1960s theologians promoting the concept of *Missio Dei* were sometimes misunderstood by churches; they took it to mean that if the mission is God's and if everything that happens in the world is part of his mission, then the churches did not need to do anything more to promote it. Echoes of extreme Calvinism resound in this argument, suggesting that the church has no part in salvation, since it is all God's doing. But if the church is seen as the body of Christ, then it shares God's work and can be seen as "a tool, an instrument through which God carries out His mission."[48]

In the Biblical record of the ministry of Jesus Christ there is a very wide-ranging spectrum of missional actions and implications. Within his preaching and teaching, discipling and story-telling, it is possible to observe references to God's concern for creation,[49] the involvement in advocacy,[50] the command to forgive,[51] the charge to be reconciled with others,[52] the example of compassion,[53] the requirement for justice,[54] and many inter-ventions with the poor, the disabled, and the sick, in all four gospels.

To what extent does this broad view of mission flow into the life of the early church? The continuity between the message and works of Jesus and the mission of the early church community was highlighted in Luke's accounts to Theophilus.[55] And in John's Gospel there is a clear connection between the mission in which the early church were engaged and the commissioning of Jesus: "As the Father has sent me, so send I you."[56]

47. Fensham, "To Be Sent." Lines 1–3
48. Vicedom, *Mission of God*, 5–6.
49. Matt 6: 28–29.
50. John 8:1–11.
51. Matt 18:35.
52. Matt 5:24.
53. Luke 15:20.
54. Luke 11:42.
55. Luke 1:1–4, Acts 1:1–9. See Senior and Stuhlmueller, *Biblical Foundations*, 256–64.
56. John 20:21.

The way in which specific Biblical mission imperatives relate to the aims of parish nursing will now be explored.

## RELEVANT THEMES IN MISSION

The research question asks how far parish nursing makes any difference to the mission of English churches and in chapter one it has been noted that the aims of parish nursing correspond to some specific themes in mission; vocation, health as wholeness, and working to extend the Kingdom of God.

## Vocation

Vocation, from the Latin *vocare*, to call, is frequently demonstrated in the lives of biblical characters from Abraham, Moses, Samuel, Isaiah and Jeremiah to the first disciples, and Saul who became Paul. In each of these cases there is a moment in time in the individual's consciousness when the voice of God was heard calling them to a specific task. In history the term has been applied to those called to what is seen as sacred rather than secular work, such as priests, monks, nuns, and missionaries. In Catholic circles this remains the traditional meaning of the term.[57] Pope John Paul II, however, spoke of a more general meaning:

> "Jesus has a specific task in life for each and every one of us. Each one of us is handpicked, called by name by Jesus! There is no-one among us who does not have a divine vocation!"[58]

Martin Luther reacted strongly against the meaning of vocation as a call to the monastic life. Instead, he saw it as a call to everyday tasks, to whatever one's station in life might be.[59] God called every Christian in whatever sphere of life they had found themselves. Thus, "the whole world could abound with services to the Lord, not only in churches but also in the home, kitchen, workshop, field."[60] The following quote contributes a useful contemporary contrast between the traditional Catholic understanding of vocation and a Lutheran one:

57. "Catholic Vocations Guide," National Religious Vocations Conference.
58. Pope John Paul II, "On Vocation."
59. Stevens, *Abolition*, 76.
60. Quoted in Feucht, *Everyone a Minister*, 80.

If vocation is God's call, there are too many Christians who expect that call to be difficult to understand. It is not uncommon to hear the assertion that God "has a personal plan for my life". The individual's responsibility then, is both to find and to follow that unique, mysterious plan. One almost conjures up images of God on a cell phone, moving from place to place, asking "can you hear me now?" with the person on the receiving end of the call desperate to find the one right place where a clear signal is possible. The Lutheran understanding of vocation offers an important corrective to this all or nothing, hit-or-miss mentality by focusing on how God is already at work in one's everyday life here and now. Within this framework, the "now" of "Can you hear me now?" suggests an incarnational commitment to any place and every place that Christians find themselves."[61]

Calvin went one step further. He agreed with Luther with regard to monasticism, but suggested that there was a predestined divine assignation to that everyday place that a Christian might occupy.[62] He interpreted the parable of the talents as relating to one's calling, and thus the divine call to a specific form of ministry as a gift to be used or buried.[63]

Fulfilling a vocation is not always a comfortable place to be. Biographies of William Carey and William Wilberforce offer accounts of people who felt strong "divine callings" upon their lives, but found that this drew them away from their peers and even into conflict with them. Such an experience resounds with Jeremiah's vocation.[64] It involves lack of fit with his peers, leading to separation as a dissenter.[65]

In Anglicanism, the term vocation is applied to those who wish to submit themselves to the given church structures in order to follow the more public leadership roles in the church. In Baptist life, although there is a strong focus on the priesthood of all believers, those presenting for accredited ministry are required to demonstrate to the local church and then a wider group of interviewers a true sense of "call" or vocation. If they can do this, and satisfy the ministerial recognition committee of their potential for ministry, they proceed to training and ordination. The word vocation has lingered in some of the professions that began as church-based initiatives,

61. Kleinhans, "Work of a Christian," 401.

62. Marshall, *Kind of Life*, 25

63. Matt 25:14–30.

64. Jer 1:1–10.

65. Thompson, "Between Text and Sermon," 66–68.

notably teaching and nursing. Yet the two terms are not synonymous. A "profession" is identified by specialist knowledge, by gated entry, internal organization, and a policed code of practice. A "vocation" has a more spiritual meaning that has been somewhat lost from teaching, nursing, medicine and social work. This is partly due to their management by secular institutions, but also because the concept of vocation has sometimes been offered as an excuse for paying someone at a lower level than their qualifications would suggest, or for demanding more hours of them than are paid.

There are strongly held differences among Baptists on the subject of vocation, as illustrated by the discussion surrounding the introduction of a new list of "Recognized Church Workers."[66] Some felt passionately that to recognize people in this way was to demote other Christians whose equally valuable time was given to other forms of service with the church or in business.

How does one "hear" a call? One suggestion comprising three dimensions offers helpful guidance:

1. We experience an inner oughtness;

2. It is bigger than ourselves;

3. It brings great satisfaction and joy.[67]

Buechner offers a statement on vocation that relates to the context of a calling: "Neither the hair shirt nor the soft berth will do; The place God calls you to is the place where your deep gladness and the world's deep hunger meet."[68] This latter reference to the mission task is taken up and further developed by Gardner in a study of four passages relating to the call of Moses, the call of Simon and Andrew, the call to the Ephesian church, and the call of Peter to the diaspora in Asia minor, resulting in a missional perspective on vocation:[69]

> God calls persons not to fulfill their life destiny as individuals, nor to supply the leadership needs of religious institutions, but to enable God's own mission to go forward in the world. God calls

66. The new proposals allowed for an additional list of Recognized Church Workers, for example, family workers, counselors and parish nurses. It was discussed in the Baptist Union Council session of March 2010 and narrowly passed, then revisited in November 2010 at which meeting it achieved much more approval.

67. Ogden, *New Reformation*, 209.

68. Buechner, *Wishful Thinking*, 95.

69. Gardner, *Vocation and Story*, 208–12.

persons to participate in a redemptive plot that has been underway
for some time, and in which yet untold episodes are beckoning.[70]

God is outworking a big transformational story in this world and to be
called is to discover how our life fits in to that big story.[71] This is true for all
followers of Christ, whatever their background. It needs to be their experience as well as their conviction and they need to be given the opportunities
to participate. The encouragement to engage in volunteering is therefore
part of the mission of the church.

Another way of looking at this theme of calling is as a double vocation—to being and to action, exemplified in the life of Jesus. Most people
are fulfilled when they are doing a job that encompasses both being and
action, and they should be encouraged to sing their song, rather than dancing to someone else's tune.[72] For many Christian nurses in a secularized
health service, the tune they are being asked to sing is not one that allows
them to be who they are and do what they feel God is calling them to do.
Whilst they may contribute to the physical healing of sick people, or promote physical or mental health, they may not speak of spiritual matters. It
is not surprising therefore that in their application forms for parish nursing
they describe a clear sense of calling.

## Health as Wholeness

There are a variety of definitions of health in addition to the one offered by
the World Health Organization: "Health is the state of complete physical,
mental and social wellbeing, not merely the absence of disease."[73] But on
what biblical basis may we include spiritual care as part of the concept of
whole-person care? Or physical and mental care as part of our concept of
spiritual care?

John Robinson points out that there is no general Hebrew term for
"body."[74] There are many terms for parts of the body, but any one of these
can also mean the whole body. The nearest word for body in the Old Testament is *Basar*, which means flesh. Neither is there a separate word for soul.

70. Ibid., 208.
71. Wright, *Mission of God,* 534.
72. Dewar, *Called or Collared,* 26.
73. World Health Organization, "Definition of Health."
74. Robinson, *Body,* 11.

So the Greek concept of body and soul being separate is not found in the Old Testament. Robinson goes on to argue that it is not present in the New Testament either. In Paul's teaching on the flesh and the body, although Paul uses two Greek words, he does not see the soul as separate. In this he follows Old Testament thinking rather than first century Greek philosophy.[75] Wilkinson sees the absence of a Hebrew word for the physical body in the Old Testament as having an implication for a Biblical concept of health:

> In view of this, we need to speak not simply of the health of the body, but of the health of the human being in all its aspects if we are to be true to the insight of the Old Testament.[76]

In my earlier work I discussed ways in which the Old Testament further illustrates the doctrine of humankind as a unified whole.[77] It was noted that the act of creation itself combined spiritual and physical elements as the Spirit of God breathed over the waters;[78] that there were instances where the physical life of God's people was inexorably intertwined with the spiritual laws given to them, for example the offering of physical sacrifices for sin;[79] and that the prophetic focus upon justice for the poor was considered a spiritual discipline as well as a physical and social act.[80]

Although there is no Biblical word for health, the nearest Old Testament word is *shalom*. It implies a deep and pervasive sense of physical mental, social, and spiritual well being, not simply in an individual sense but in relationship with God.[81] Wilkinson notes six Old Testament characteristics of health: wellbeing, righteousness, obedience, strength, fertility, and longevity.[82] From them he chooses "well-being" as the closest definition of health in the Old Testament.[83] However, throughout the narrative of the life of God's people there are degrees of well-being; people are not perfectly whole all of the time.

---

75. Ibid., 17–33.

76. Wilkinson, *Bible and Healing*, 10.

77. Wordsworth, "Parish Nursing," 22–29.

78. Gen 1:1–2.

79. Lev 4:22–23.

80. Amos 5:21.

81. Ps 29:11.

82. Wilkinson, *Bible and Healing*, 11.

83. Ibid., 16.

A biblical understanding of wholeness, then, is a dynamic concept, that includes moving towards a relationship with God. In this it is different from a contemporary worldview of holism that may or may not include reference to a higher being. For parish nursing this is a significant differential that will be explored further in the next section.

In the New Testament we find a similar lack of any one word being translated "health." Greek words used are *hugies,* which means soundness, balance; *eirene* which is often translated as peace, meaning peace with God, others or self; *zoe* meaning life in all its fullness; *teleios,* meaning perfect, mature; *soteria* meaning safe and sound; and the verb *sozo* meaning deliverance from a dangerous and threatening situation.[84] There were many occasions in the ministry of Jesus when he healed people and at the same time addressed their spiritual condition, either by forgiving sin,[85] or encouraging faith.[86] The incarnation, passion, suffering and death and resurrection of Jesus imply a togetherness of physical and spiritual being; the concept of wholeness of body mind and spirit was present in the writings of the early church;[87] and in the eschatological passages there is a perspective on future wholeness.[88] Wilkinson expresses a New Testament concept of health as life, blessedness (as in the beatitudes), holiness, and maturity.[89]

Judaism and Christianity are not alone in emphasizing the importance of a wholistic view of humankind. In the field of complementary and alternative medicine, there is also a desire to move away from dualism. Roger Hurding notes that most cultures and religions have some concept of wholeness, as a state of health and completeness that is generally felt to be desirable, if not attainable, and describes the central tenets concerning pathways to wholeness in Hinduism and Buddhism, Confucianism and Taoism, and Islam.[90] He highlights the commonality these have with Christianity in identifying the now and the not yet, the process and the goal of wholeness. But Hurding also emphasizes the unique claims of Christianity with regard to wholeness as "the daily, life-changing engagement with God

---

84. Ibid., 22–26.

85. Luke 7:44–50.

86. Luke 8:43–48.

87. Rom 12:1–2.

88. Rev 21:4.

89. Ibid., 26–30.

90. Hurding, *Pathways to Wholeness,* 12.

and neighbor, and the promise of eventual fulfillment as a new people in a new heaven and earth."[91]

This biblical view of embodied wholeness is quite different from the Greek concept of the soul as a separate entity that leads to dualism; the separation between the spiritual which is seen as good and immortal, and the physical which is seen as imperfect and mortal. It is also quite different from the praxis of the National Health Service, which tends to compartmentalize physical aspects of health care from mental, emotional, and spiritual aspects, and indeed even categorizes physical symptoms and treatment in separate and divisive specialties.

Such a view of wholeness concurs with that put forward by the Christian Medical Commission's study group in 1981. Theologians met with physicians from around the world over a five-year period and the results were published in 1981.[92] They are summarized in the following statement:

> Medicine must not only abandon the separation of body soul and spirit but must also understand the human person as a being in relationship to other persons, to the environment, and to God.[93]

Abigail Rian-Evans has examined a Biblical view of health from a background in both medicine and theology. She has pleaded for a radical reconstruction of our understanding of healing and healers. She has identified the following aspects which she suggests are unique to the Judeo-Christian tradition:

1. It is based on a doctrine of humankind as a unity, both within us and with our environment and community;

2. Its definitions of health as wholeness and of sickness as brokenness include a spiritual dimension;

3. It orients to health instead of sickness;

4. Its primary goal is other's health, not our own;

5. It broadens healing to include any activity that moves us toward wholeness;

6. It understands healers as persons who move us toward healing.[94]

91. Ibid., 27.

92. McGilvray, *Quest for Health.*

93. Benn and Senturias, "Health, Healing, and Wholeness," 18.

94. Rian Evans, *Redeeming Marketplace Medicine*, 67.

"Too often," says Rian-Evans, "we reduce health to bodily well-being and confine salvation to the state of the soul."[95] This stands as a challenge to the UK church's gradual withdrawal from physical health issues as the NHS has taken on these responsibilities. Have some sections of the church become unwittingly overtaken by a dualistic tendency? Do they focus on the spiritual life to the exclusion of physical wellbeing, and do they maybe even have a preoccupation with the spiritual and miraculous aspects of healing to the exclusion of more mundane physical health interventions? If so, perhaps the appointment of a parish nurse might help to correct that imbalance.

## The Extension of God's Kingdom

The biblical narrative shows that God promised his kingdom in the world firstly through engaging with the people of Israel, then introducing it through the ministry, death and resurrection of Jesus, then nurturing it through the obedience of the first disciples and then spreading it across the world through the church. Throughout the Bible there is the eschatological anticipation that one day his kingdom will come in full. In the meantime, as has been seen, the church is invited to share in God's mission task of extending that kingdom.

A parish nurse's clients come from both within and outside of the community of believers. The NMC code of practice dictates that a nurse cannot refuse to offer care to anyone because of their beliefs, race, or gender.[96] In appointing a parish nurse, therefore the church is opening up to the possibility of engaging with people who are not yet believers, and may never want to be so. The nurse works with them in a way that is respectful of their faith or non-faith position. How then does parish nursing sit with the Biblical imperatives on extending God's Kingdom? Or with the Biblical view of wholeness which includes a relationship with God?

In the gospels, Jesus' ministry to the gentiles is exceptional rather than normal and does not usually involve taking the initiative.[97] His focus on the house of Israel is particularly obvious in Matthew. For example, where

95. Ibid., 73.

96. "Code of Practice." The only exception to this is in the case of someone requiring legal abortion, where under law the nurse may refer to someone else if she/he feels unable to participate in the termination because of conscience.

97. Köstenberger and O'Brien, Salvation, 94.

he sends out the twelve he instructs them not to go among the gentiles.[98] And in Jesus' discourse about the sheep and the goats the king says, "As you did it to the least of these brothers of mine, you did it to me."[99] The context of the story is the final judgment, and the timing of it is close to the end of Jesus' earthly ministry. He may well have been aware of the dangers facing the disciples and of the need to encourage them to care for one another as they suffered in his name. But to whom is Jesus is referring in his use of the term "brothers," and "the least of these"? Is this an implication that charitable works done in the name of Christ should be restricted in any way? Goldsmith, writing from a Jewish Christian background, suggests that this refers to those who follow Jesus and are in union with him.[100] Hendriksen offers the definition "all those saved by grace regardless of nationality, race etc."[101] Wright notes that Jesus has "earlier defined his brothers (and sisters) as those who do the will of my Father in heaven."[102] Sider is uncertain about the exclusivity of such an interpretation. He writes:

> Even if the primary reference of these words is to poor believers, other aspects of Jesus' teaching not only permit but require us to extend the meaning of Matthew chapter twenty-five to both believers and unbelievers who are poor and oppressed.[103]

Clearly, the disciples are being instructed to care for believers, but it should be added that they are not prevented from caring for unbelievers. Indeed, there is much evidence to suggest that a wider biblical reading offers a more inclusive attitude both to those who will respond to the gospel of Christ and to the beneficiaries of Christian charitable works. For in the same gospel Jesus commends the centurion's faith, and gives us a glimpse of the future participation of gentiles in the kingdom of God.[104] A similar statement is made in relation to the parable of the wicked tenants of the vineyard.[105] And in Matthew there are other gospel references to the need to be present in the world outside the believing community, for example,

98. Matt 10:5.

99. Matt 25:40.

100. Goldsmith, *Matthew and Mission*, 178.

101. Hendriksen, *Gospel of Matthew*, 886.

102. Wright, *Matthew for Everyone*, 142.

103. Sider, *Rich Christians*, 73.

104. Matt 8:10. Jesus anticipates this by his actions in Luke 17:18, and in John 4:7, where he engages with Samaritan people.

105. Matt 21:33–46.

the call to be salt and light in the world.[106] Indeed, Matthew makes it clear that after the resurrection, the mission to extend the kingdom of God was to go beyond the Jewish nation. At the end of his gospel there is the great commission, the charge to go and make disciples of all nations, including Israel.[107] Luke, writing with gentiles as potential readers in mind, includes references to a centurion's household,[108] Jonah and the Ninevites,[109] and the Samaritan healed of leprosy, as examples of Jesus' ministry and teaching as it affected those who were not Jews by birth. He even uses the example of a compassionate Samaritan to teach Jews about true neighborliness. And he records Jesus as instructing his disciples to "love your enemies and do good to them."[110] John has Jesus talking with a Samaritan woman, and many of her friends coming to faith in Him.[111]

How are these examples of Jesus' concern for those outside the Jewish faith relevant to today's English church?

Senior and Stuhlmueller examine the change that occurred in early Christian history when the largely Jewish community of believers followed the instruction of Jesus and widened its vision to include mission to gentile people.[112] They compare this to the position of the western church today, where centuries of Christendom have instilled a culture that does not engage effectively with people of other faiths or none. This is of great importance to our research question because, unlike the days when charitable works were done against a background of Christian dominance, parish nurses now work in a post-Christendom society. There are many English churches that, as a local entity, have very little if any dealings with the community that immediately surrounds them. Christians often work individually and sometimes anonymously in England's secular environment, but they face restrictions on what can be said about faith in their business life. How then may the work to which the disciples were commissioned by Jesus, be continued?

In Luke, when seventy-two disciples are sent out on a mission they are to bring peace, to eat with host families, to heal the sick and to say that the

106. Matt 5:13–16.
107. Matt 28:19.
108. Luke 7:1–10.
109. Luke 11:29–32.
110. Luke 6:35.
111. John 4:1–42.
112. Senior and Stuhlmueller, *Biblical Foundations,* 157.

Kingdom of God is near.[113] This time although the towns and villages will probably have been Jewish, there is no specific prohibition on working with others. This gospel, together with the book of Acts provides a much clearer focus on the mission of Jesus and the church with gentiles. Although as already noted, Jesus concentrated on his ministry within Israel, His universal mission begins after his death and resurrection. The last words of Jesus on earth are the sending of the disciples as his witnesses to Jerusalem, Judaea, Samaria and the ends of the earth.[114] That work is continued by the church in Acts and in particular through Paul's missionary journeys, the first of which results in gentile converts in South Galatia.[115]

In Paul's subsequent letter to the Galatians, the gentile mission was seen as a fulfillment of the Abrahamic covenant:

> The scripture foresaw that God would justify the gentiles by faith, and announced the gospel in advance to Abraham: "All nations will be blessed through you." So those who have faith are blessed along with Abraham, the man of faith.[116]

Wright's perspective on this is that "the things God said to Abraham become the ultimate agenda for God's own mission (blessing the nations) and the things Abraham did in response become the proximate model for our mission (faith and obedience)."[117]

The phrase "extending the Kingdom of God" may therefore be understood as a continuation of the missional purpose of God reaching out to humankind, begun with Abraham, supremely achieved in Christ and now being demonstrated and proclaimed wherever it is not yet experienced and not yet known. That work is mostly done by his church. It includes the transforming of lives, the bringing of justice, the relief of poverty, the ministry of healing and reconciliation, the bringing of shalom, the care for creation, the increase in works of service, and the knowledge of God's word. Many local churches will design mission statements that seek to address these objectives. They may try to achieve their aims through church

---

113. Luke 10:8–9.

114. Acts 1:8.

115. Acts 13.

116. Gal 3:7–9.

117. Wright, *Mission of God*, 208.

planting and evangelism, or by developing enabling structures like local home groups.[118]

In the light of all that is good in England's welfare state, does this extension of God's Kingdom only happen through the church? For example, if a secular body sets up a clinic in a local church building to serve the neighborhood, but without any reference to faith or the gospel, is that not also extending God's Kingdom? There is some debate among evangelical theologians about the value of such work relative to the redemptive order and the church. Chester quotes some notable missiologists who see God at work beyond the church:

> The kingdom comes wherever Jesus overcomes the evil one. This happens, (or ought to happen) in fullest measure in the church. But it also happens in society."[119]

> Not infrequently, if we have eyes to see this, God is advancing his kingdom through those who may not recognize this, but whose quest for justice and wholeness, for liberty and community, is contributing towards the kingdom's advance."[120]

He points out however that in the New Testament extension of the Kingdom of God happens only when Christ is acknowledged as King, and full salvation is only brought through the cross. He reminds us that even where God is seen to be working in and through people beyond the church, that work should not be separated from the gospel, the good news of salvation through repentance and faith in Christ. The purpose of the church is to extend the kingdom in its complete form, both by action and word.[121] The kingdom comes by healing and telling.[122] A biblical understanding of wholeness includes a relationship with God. By implication, this means that those who do not yet have that relationship are not yet whole. Clearly, though, God loves them and wants them to be whole.[123]

Alongside this it should be noted that in the Biblical record, such relationship with God is offered as a choice, rather than a compulsion. People are not pressurized into opening themselves to the kingdom of

---

118. Kirk, *What is Mission?* 219.

119. Bosch, *Witness*, 209

120. Murray, *Church Planting*, 43.

121. Chester, *Good News*, 73.

122. Luke 10:9.

123. John 3:16.

God. This is true in the Old Testament, where response to God's way was optional both for individuals and for communities; and in the New Testament, where some people, like the rich man who went away sadly in Matt 19:22, chose not to follow Christ. Although there is a reference to force in Matt 11:12, it is in the context of the relationship between John's ministry and the coming of the Kingdom of God.[124] John's question comes from a place of impotence, a prison, where he is seeking some form of confirmation that Jesus really is the Messiah. Interestingly, Jesus does not respond to John's question about his identity with a forceful affirmation of his own divinity and power. Rather, he refers to the natural power of the Kingdom spreading across the country by means of miraculous signs. And in verse 14, Matthew includes the phrase "if you are willing to accept it," indicating that even though the message was powerful, Jesus was offering his hearers the gift of choice.

Furthermore, in the gospels, understanding and maturity in faith may take some time to develop. This is evident in the references to Nicodemus in John's gospel.[125] His questions indicate that he was exploring faith in Christ, but was not yet a fully committed follower. There is no Biblical authority to use pressure of any kind in extending God's Kingdom. It is especially important to remember this when dealing with those who are vulnerable.

In the 2010 Lausanne meetings at Cape Town, a commitment to world mission was made:

> All our mission must reflect the integration of evangelism and committed engagement in the world, both being ordered and driven by the whole biblical revelation of the gospel of God . . . Integral mission is the proclamation and demonstration of the gospel. It is not simply that evangelism and social involvement are to be done alongside each other. Rather, in integral mission our proclamation has social consequences as we call people to love and repentance in all areas of life. And our social involvement has evangelistic consequences as we bear witness to the transforming grace of Jesus Christ. If we ignore the world, we betray the word of God, which sends us out to serve the world. If we ignore the Word of God, we have nothing to bring to the world.[126]

124. Matt 11:12.

125. John 3:2, John 7:50–52, and John 19:39. See also Senior and Stuhlmueller, *Biblical Foundations*, 256–64.

126. Lausanne, "Cape Town Commitment," 11–12.

In attempting to bring shalom to the world, Christians are offering people a relationship with God as well as helping them with the mental, physical, and social aspects of life. They are not offering ease, riches, or a life of luxury. They are inviting people to join the journey of following Christ, which at times may be tough, demanding and sacrificial. It will cause them to examine their own lives, and their relationships with others. It will invite them to learn how to worship God. This is the way to a Biblical view of health.

## THE MISSION OF AN ENGLISH CHURCH

What then is the mission of a local English church? Is it the pursuance of a spiritual experience of conversion for all with whom it comes in contact? Is it the call to a more devoted life, or more authentic discipleship? Is it the engagement in works of service in the local community? If so, is that work to be done in the name of the church of Christ or can it be offered under some other name?

Around the community there will be numerous examples of people acting within the will of God. Whilst they may not be members of any church, they may hold to the values of Christ, or indeed to those elements of other faiths that coincide with the values of God's Kingdom. They could perhaps be seen as the "men and women of peace" in our communities, referred to by Jesus in Luke 10:5. Disciples of Jesus may stay with them and work from and in their places of influence. But that does not exempt those disciples from offering the whole message of Christ in those environments.

Members of the church may be encouraged to live out their faith in whatever context they are placed, being salt and light in the world, demonstrating the fruit of the God's Spirit in their lives and rooting for the justice of God wherever they can. Some may be called to work in very difficult places and will need all the prayer support that the church can muster. Where they are placed by virtue of their employment under secular rule, the instruction of Jesus is to "give to Caesar that which is Caesar's and to God that which is God's."[127] Whilst they may offer their skills, their transformed lives and their Christian presence in those circumstances it is difficult for them to share their faith with others in a verbal way.

But the task of the church is to share the whole gospel of God, not just part of it. It follows therefore that where the secular context prohibits the

127. Matt. 22:21.

full expression of the gospel the task of the church is to offer not just the remaining part, for that leads to a form of dualism. Rather, as far as she is able, the church must seek to engage fully with the needs of the community around her and do so from a distinctively Christian perspective. So where church members are engaged for much of their time by secular organizations, could they not be encouraged to think about how their particular skills could also be employed in the name of the church for at least a few hours a month?

Such a mission task requires resources of time and money. In the parable of the talents, there is a clear implication that the recipients of gifts are accountable for the way in which they invested them.[128] Lines of accountability must be in place so that the resources available are used to greatest effect. Christian believers must demonstrate holy lives, as far as they are able, and support networks will help to monitor this.

How shall such work be evaluated? In the world's eyes, evaluation depends on measurable client outcomes. For the church, ultimate accountability is to Christ Himself as illustrated in Matthew's account of the sheep and the goats.[129] In that story, as in the parable of the Good Samaritan, the implication is that people are accountable for what they did, rather than for the resulting client outcomes.[130] Yet Jesus appears to take note of the response of the ten healed of leprosy in Luke 17.[131]

It has been seen that nothing must be done by compulsion, choice being offered in all circumstances. The Holy Spirit is the one who converts people and that whilst Christians may long for signs of transformed lives, they cannot control a person's response to the gospel.[132] Therefore any evaluation of a church's mission needs to encompass more than the number of conversions or baptisms seen.

If the missional task is seen as the call to more authentic discipleship, then in a missional church people will live and act more like Christ. The highest professional standards and care must be offered so that the name of Christ is not dishonored. Any evaluation of a church's mission should therefore also include attention to detail and the standard of care given should be higher than that expected in the world.

128. Luke 19:12–27.
129. Matt. 25:31–46.
130. Luke 10:1–37.
131. Luke 17:17–19
132. John 3:6, John 16:13, Rom 8:9.

## SUMMARY

We have explored the concept of mission because the research question demands an understanding of what is meant by the mission of an English church. Historical, theological, and biblical influences on missiological activity have been examined. Greater focus has been applied to the themes of vocation, wholeness, and the extension of God's Kingdom, because these have a particular bearing on the work of a parish nurse. It has been argued that the mission of a local church includes

a. the release and deployment of all members who experience a sense of God's call to ministries of various kinds;

b. involvement in activities that promote physical, mental, social and spiritual health;

c. the extension of God's reign, and the offer of His salvation amongst people that do not yet know him;

d. respect for the God-given gift of freewill that offers choices to people of all backgrounds and faiths;

e. and the integration of evangelism and social engagement in such a way that both engaging with the world's needs and proclaiming the word of God are part of the same task.

The aim of this missional work is to bless all peoples by pointing to the possibility of salvation through Christ and transformation of individual and communal life; by working with them in a respectful way towards healing and reconciliation; and by furthering the divine values of justice, peace, and concern for God's creation.

We now turn to the crucial question. How far does the appointment of a parish nurse to work with a local church congregation meet any of the five criteria outlined above, and how far does it contribute to the blessing of all peoples within the scope of these divine purposes?

In order to elicit a response to this question, it is necessary to find out more about the way in which parish nurses engage with volunteers: the extent of the involvement of parish nurses in each of the four areas of health-promoting activities; the degree to which parish nurses work beyond the church community; whether or not parish nursing interventions help people move towards a saving faith in Christ; the measure of respect for freewill choice that is offered through parish nursing; and the ways in which social action and discussion about faith and prayer are integrated in the practice of parish nursing. The next chapter describes the way in which a methodology for exploring this was developed.

# 4

# Identification of a Method
# to Address the Research Question

HAVING DESCRIBED AND DISCUSSED the potential contribution of parish nursing, and engaged with the missiological debate about what might constitute the mission of a local church, I now turn to the question of how a practical methodology was designed.

The research question was "How far does parish nursing make a difference to the mission of an English church?" Traditionally, mission effectiveness has been measured by the numbers of converts to the Christian faith or new attendees to the church. If these were simply to be counted, they would form part of the answer, and this would be of interest, not least because those new people may then become engaged in the mission task of the church. But that would be a limited perspective, because it has been argued that the church's mission task is much more comprehensive than simply attracting new members. So although these numbers may be noted, they have not been considered as primary indicators in the search for answers to the question. Rather, this study needed to look closely at the missional activity that had been stimulated by the appointment of a parish nurse to the ministry team.

Therefore, I searched for some way of measuring that difference against the five missional criteria identified in chapter three, and some means of assessing the extent to which it met those criteria within the divine purposes discussed there. To recollect, the five criteria were:

a. the release and deployment of all members who experience a sense of God's call to ministries of various kinds;

b. involvement in activities that promote physical, mental, social, and spiritual health;

c. the extension of God's reign, and the offer of his salvation amongst people that do not yet know him;

d. respect for the God-given gift of freewill that offers choices to people of all backgrounds and faiths;

e. the integration of evangelism and social engagement in such a way that both engaging with the world's needs and proclaiming the word of God are part of the same task.

For the purpose of designing a methodology, nine questions were devised that related directly to each of the above criteria.

So, for criterion (a), question one was developed: "How do parish nurses engage with volunteers?" For criterion (b), questions: two, three, four, and five: "What is the involvement of parish nurses in each of the four areas of health-promoting activities; physical, mental, community and spiritual health?" For criterion (c) questions six and seven: "What is the degree to which parish nurses work beyond the church community?" and "Do parish nursing interventions help people move towards a saving faith in Christ?" For criterion (d), question eight: "What respect for freewill and choice is offered through the ministry of parish nursing?" And for criterion (e), question nine: "In what ways are social action and evangelism integrated in the practice of parish nursing?"

A mixed method approach was taken and the path chosen was one that focused on qualitative case study research with some complementary quantitative survey material. The reasons for this decision and the ways in which it was implemented will be explained in this chapter.

## THE SAMPLE

Parish nurse projects happen in a variety of churches from different denominations and in diverse communities. If just one or two of these were chosen and examined in detail, the results of the study might be replicated in a church of a similar size and denomination to the case studied, but would not necessarily be the same in a different context. The sample therefore needed to be wider than one or two projects and needed to include churches from more than one denomination.

Parish nurse projects take time to become active. After the one week introductory course, the parish nurse returns to the church to share some of the principles learnt and seek to recruit a team of supporting individuals who will help to identify the most appropriate channels for parish nursing ministry around that church. There may be some significant changes to be brought about relating to the congregation's view of health ministry and wholeness, as well as the need to develop good working relationships with other primary health care providers. It is therefore difficult to make any valid evaluation of practice in the first six months. So in order for the extent of any impact to be reliably assessed, a church needed to have had an active parish nurse ministry for a substantial amount of time. For this reason, it was felt that eighteen months should be the minimum amount of experience offered in any of the projects that were to be examined.

## Subjectivity

The most important issue that had to be addressed in designing a methodology was that of subjectivity. In my role as a founder and UK Coordinator of Parish Nursing Ministries UK, I naturally wanted to be able to demonstrate clearly that parish nursing has something to contribute to the mission of UK churches and I was in grave danger of influencing this study in a way that would yield biased results. Yet as a reflective practitioner I also had to critically evaluate the effects of the movement that I had started, and this was and is a key element in any research linked to professional practice. I therefore had to devise a methodology that gave me enough distance from the subjects of the research to enable a degree of objectivity, whilst all the time acknowledging my own potential influence on what was reported. This tension is otherwise known as reflexivity: "the process of critical self-reflection carried out by the researcher throughout the research process that enables her to monitor and respond to her contribution to the proceedings."[1]

Those who knew most about the extent of the work they were involved in were the nurses themselves. Yet many of them were also passionate about what they were doing and had an interest in describing their work in a positive light. It was therefore decided in the first instance not to include

1. Swinton and Mowat, *Practical Theology,* 59.

them in an interview method, but rather to work simply with their ministers, who would have a greater understanding of missiological issues and a broader view of the extent to which their churches were engaging in mission. Ministers were therefore chosen as both the subjects for the pre-interview surveys, and as the primary interviewees. In that way it was hoped to gain a more objective view of the practice and perhaps pick up any of the more negative factors.

In the parish nurse church sample, these ministers were not well known to the researcher. In most cases it was the first meeting with them. In the control group sample, it was requested that all the surveys be completed by ministers rather than other members of the congregation. This was in order to stay as close as possible to the conditions surrounding the pre-interview survey for the ministers of the parish nurse churches. About 15 percent of the control group ministers that submitted surveys were personally known, 40 percent were known in a formal capacity, and 45 percent not known at all.

At the time of beginning this research, there were twenty-nine churches that had been engaged with a parish nurse ministry for more than eighteen months in England. The majority of these were either Anglican or Baptist churches, with just two or three from other denominations. In order to gain some kind of perspective on the extent of the effect on their mission, at least twelve of these ministers would need to be interviewed. But another challenge to the subjectivity of the research was encountered: as UK Coordinator for parish nursing I knew which churches had the most active projects and it would have been very easy to select the ones that were likely to produce the most positive results. A more randomized approach was therefore sought: all twenty-nine churches that fulfilled the eighteen-month criteria were contacted, and all that volunteered to take part were engaged in the study, regardless of their strength, weakness, or denomination.

## The Participants

With a field of only twenty-nine churches from a variety of contexts to approach, it was not possible to conduct a fully randomized study and be sure of recruiting twelve willing participants who might comprise a large enough sample to offer significant findings. Instead letters were written enclosing stamped addressed envelopes to the ministers of all twenty-nine of these churches asking them whether or not they would be willing to fill in a questionnaire, and whether or not they would agree to be interviewed.[2] The problem with this approach was that responses were only received from those interested enough to want to take part, but at least there was a lesser possibility of bias than if I had chosen the subjects. In the event, fifteen of the ministers replied positively. Interestingly, these responding ministers reflected the same proportion of denominational identity as the field of twenty-nine: seven Anglican, seven Baptist, and one Evangelical church. All were in based in England, but spread around from the Northwest to London through the Midlands and from Yorkshire to East Anglia.

M1 was the male vicar of a large Anglican church in an affluent, medium-sized rural market town, with a fairly high church style of worship. The congregation regularly numbered over 200; they were majority white in ethnicity, and the average age was sixty-three, which was a little older than the average age of the population in that town. Their parish nurse had worked voluntarily for the church for around twelve hours per week for four years, in addition to her part-time NHS community nurse post.

M2 was the male minister of a Baptist church in a deprived multicultural area to the east of a large city. The regular congregation numbered between one hundred and one hundred and forty-nine. They were of mixed ethnicity, West Indian and white Caucasian but with very few Asian attendees. The average age was forty-three. Their parish nurse had come from a different church and had worked with them on a voluntary basis for around eighteen hours per week for eighteen months. She also worked part-time as an NHS practice nurse in a neighboring part of the area around the church.

M3 was the male minister of a Baptist church in a deprived part of a seaside town. Many of the surrounding houses were large and divided into privately rented flats. There was a regular congregation of one hundred to one hundred and forty-nine. The attendees were majority white, with an average age of forty. The parish nurse had worked for the church six hours per week on a voluntary basis for eighteen months, and was also employed by the local hospital part-time. Shortly after the research was completed she retired away from the area, and despite a strong desire to replace her, at the time of writing the church has not found another nurse.

M4 was the male minister of a Baptist church with an ethnically mixed congregation in a widely multicultural inner city area. Three other ethnically-based congregations also used the building. The average age

2. See Appendix 1.

of the congregation was around forty. The parish nurse worked on a paid basis for the church's family centre for two days a week. She was also employed by the church for a further two days as a pastoral worker, and by the NHS as a children's specialist for one day per week. She had been in post for five years.

M5 was the female vicar of an Anglican church on a large council housing estate in a market town. The majority white congregation, of between fifty and ninety-nine regular attendees, were of an average age of sixty, which matched the surrounding community population profile. The parish nurse had retired from NHS community nursing and had been working for the church twelve hours per week on a voluntary basis for three years.

M6 was the female vicar of an Anglican church in the suburban commuter area of a large city. Her majority-white congregation averaged one hundred and fifty to one hundred and ninety-nine regular attendees with a high worship style and a robed choir. The average age was around sixty-four, which roughly matched the average age of the local population. The parish nurse was employed as a staff nurse at the local hospital and had also worked ten hours a week voluntarily for the church for the preceding four years.

M7 was the male vicar of a benefice of isolated rural parishes. Usual congregations were of between fifty and ninety-nine attendees, majority white in ethnicity, with an average age of sixty-five. His wife was the parish nurse, and she worked in the benefice for nine hours a week of which two hours a week were paid from a church fund restricted to parish nursing activities. She had been doing this for five years, alongside various other part-time health-related activities.

M8 was the male minister of a Baptist church in a large village. The congregation size was regularly over one hundred, some of whom came from surrounding villages or a nearby town. They were majority white in ethnicity, matching the local population, and the average age was thirty-five. The parish nurse was also practice nurse in the same village and had been working for the church on a voluntary basis for two years, on average around six hours a week.

M9 was the male vicar of an Anglican church on a deprived council housing estate with some private terraced housing to the east of a city. The average age of the majority-white congregation was thirty-five. This church had a regular attendance on Sundays of fifty to ninety-nine, but the church building had undergone some refurbishment with a coffee shop at the street entrance that attracted visitors of all ages during its opening hours each weekday. The parish nurse had worked three days a week for the church on a voluntary basis for eighteen months.

M10 was the female vicar of a rural Anglican church with fifty to ninety-nine regular attendees. The average age was around sixty-six. Both the community and the congregation were almost entirely white Caucasian in origin. The parish nurse had worked for the church for eighteen months for seven hours per week on a voluntary basis and was also employed as a hospital nurse. She had begun to explore possible links with the Methodist church in the same village. One year after the research was completed this nurse retired and because there was no one to replace her, the project closed.

M11 was the male minister of a large Baptist church in an affluent suburban commuter area. His majority white congregation consisted of over one hundred and fifty regular attendees, with an average age of thirty-nine. The parish nurse had worked six hours a week for the church on a voluntary basis for the last two years. She also had her own business, not connected with nursing.

M12 was the male minister of a Baptist church in an industrial port. He had recently come to the church, and stated that he had been attracted to it in part because of its outreach in health ministry. The majority white congregation of fifty to ninety-nine regular attendees was of an average age of fifty-eight. The parish nurse had started as a volunteer three years previously, but at the time of the interview was being paid by the church for two days a week. She was also employed by the NHS as a part-time community nurse. After the research was completed, she was offered a new full-time post with the NHS in a different part of the county and so resigned from the parish nurse post. She was subsequently replaced by a nurse from the local Methodist church.

M13 was a retired male vicar working as a non-stipendiary assistant minister in an Anglican church in a large fairly affluent village. The average age of the congregation was sixty-five and, like the community around them, they were majority white in ethnicity. The parish nurse had been a district nurse in the same area for many years and was well known in the community. She had been serving as a parish nurse on a voluntary basis for eight hours a week for four years, but had just retired from the NHS and was now working fifteen hours a week for the church.

M14 was the male minister of a village Baptist church with a regular, majority white congregation of between fifty and ninety-nine, situated in an isolated rural area. The average age of the attendees was fifty-eight. The parish nurse had been working with the church for two years at the time of interview. She was paid by the church for fifteen hours a week, gave five hours a week on a voluntary basis, and worked as an NHS practice nurse in the area for the rest of the time.

M15 was the male minister of an Independent Evangelical church in a large village. The attendance on Sundays averaged between fifty and ninety-nine people from the local area and like the population, they were largely white Caucasian in origin. The average age was forty-five. This church had two parish nurses, both quite different in background but working in a complementary way. One was a retired health visitor who had been working for the church for five years, and the other for two years. Both gave two days each on a voluntary basis. The longer serving parish nurse took part in the interview, but the other was away at the time of the visit.

It can therefore be seen that there was some variety of context and size in the sample that responded to the invitation to participate: these ministers were from rural, market town, urban, and suburban areas; most congregations were medium-sized, all with regular attendances of over fifty, but there were also larger congregations. Three churches offered some payment for parish nursing hours, though the rest paid their parish nurses' expenses only. Although there was no question concerning theological stance, it became clear during the visits that four of the Anglican churches were from a traditional, moderately high church background, and two were more evangelical in their outlook. The Baptist churches varied in worship style but all appeared to be moderately evangelical in their doctrine and practice. None were particularly charismatic or reformed in their teaching. It was decided to interview all fifteen ministers, in order to avoid bias in choosing specific projects on the basis of their perceived fruitfulness.

During the first set of interviews it became clear that there was a need to engage with more subjects than the ministers, partly because they were not party to all that was happening in their project, and partly because they too may have had a reason to "talk up" the outcomes. So in order to achieve a corroborated body of evidence the nurses in all of these fifteen projects were also interviewed, without the ministers being present. In addition to this on two occasions an attempt was made to conduct interviews with a focus group of service-users; but it was almost impossible to gather sufficient numbers of them together for a recorded interview, and their responses were very stilted and repetitive due to the presence of the microphone. The exercise was not repeated. However there was an additional source of information about the activities of UK parish nurses from a wider group of churches that submitted annual statistics to Parish Nursing Ministries UK as a routine requirement and this provided a further useful contribution during the period of the study.

Some form of background comparative evidence seemed desirable alongside this qualitative work, but the need for the nurse to have been practicing for eighteen months meant that it was not possible to conduct interviews before and after they had begun working as a parish nurse. This comparative background was therefore provided by a further self-generated sample of ministers: internet or paper surveys were offered to Anglican, Baptist, and Evangelical churches through several regional and diocesan mailings, and the responses came from a range of rural, suburban, urban, small, medium, and large churches with different theological backgrounds.

## INSTRUMENTATION

For the qualitative approach, the instrument of choice was a one-to-one interview with the minister of the church. A one-to-one interview is a common component in naturalistic enquiry, often used in unstructured and open-ended ways, but may be designed with some structure if the researcher is experienced in the field and is looking for insights into specific questions.[3] A semi-structured questionnaire gave a framework within which to compare case studies but also allowed the interviewee the freedom to describe incidents or problems that were not direct answers. Follow up questions could be asked by the interviewer if she sensed that an interviewee might want to say more about a particular topic.

It was decided to collect prior information to that which would be contributed through the interview method, so that more could be gleaned from those who preferred a written form of communication to a verbal one, and any surprising responses could be clarified during the interview. A written questionnaire was designed and sent to all fifteen ministers. This offered the possibility of more definitive answers to relevant questions and gave options for identifying the church's most commonly performed missional activities together with a view on whether or not the parish nurse

3. Depoy and Gitlin, *Introduction to Research*, 222.

was involved with these. And to help with the task of collecting comparative information, the same tool was used to extract similar information from the wider sample of churches but without the questions specifically relating to the nurses.

Statistical data relating to the interventions of more parish nurses across the UK was gleaned from their annual returns for 2010.

I therefore had four instruments: the pre-interview written questionnaire for participants; the similar written questionnaire for churches without parish nurses; the semi-structured interviews; and the statistical returns from a wider group of parish nurses.

## The Questionnaires

The first design of the written questionnaire was tested with several colleagues and found wanting. It was too long, too general and contained phrases and words that could be differently understood. It needed a complete rethink. A search was then made for a tried and tested model that could be used to identify different strands of missional activity.

Attempts to measure a church's mission activity have formed part of several models for church "health" assessment that have been offered to UK churches in the last twenty-five years.[4] Some, for example, "Natural Church Development," focus mainly on the life of the church community and have very little reference to service in the local community.[5] But one of these, "The Healthy Churches' Handbook," focuses on the quality of the church's life rather than just the numbers attending, and centers around seven characteristic "marks" of health.[6] Some of these marks relate directly to the mission of the church, for example:

Mark 2. An outward looking focus, with a whole life rather than a church life concern: Deeply rooted in the local community, working in partnership with other denominations, faiths, secular groups and networks; passionate and prophetic about justice and

4. For example, the Baptist Union AIM program, Baptist Union Mission Consultation project, Natural Church Development, TEAR Fund Church Community and Change, and Healthy Church UK.

5. Schwarz and Schalk, *Natural Church Development*, 119.

6. Warren, *Healthy Churches Handbook*. The seven marks of a healthy church are that it: 1) Is energized by faith. 2) Has an outward looking focus. 3) Seeks to find out what God wants. 4) Faces the cost of change and growth. 5) Operates as a community. 6) Makes room for all. 7) Does a few things and does them well.

peace, locally and globally; makes connections between faith and daily living; responds to human need by loving service.

A scoring guide of 1–6 is offered to church members as a way of assessing the mission life of a church in these respects. As such it is a useful tool, though quite subjective, and the answers would reflect the degree to which each church member has knowledge of the church's involvement in the community. This method of church health assessment was thought to be too generalized for the purpose of the research.

"Community Mission" is a joint project between Livability and Tear Fund designed to help churches relate more closely to their communities, and they too provide a model for assessment.[7] This is based on ten core factors: presence, impact, partnership, heart, ownership, leadership, roots, adaptability, finance and vision. All ten factors are placed around a 360-degree wheel diagram. This enables a church or project to show change in any one of these areas by inviting participants to place a score from zero to ten at various stages of the project. The researcher felt that while this might be a very helpful way of looking at the measurement of change for an individual project or intensive case-study approach, it was not such a good model for examining a variety of mission interventions in fifteen different churches. Something more specific was needed, preferably something that had been tried and tested in other contexts.

A comprehensive documentation tool, listing core parish nurse interventions, had been developed in America. It had been used for the purpose of enabling parish nurses to record and evaluate their work.[8] In that study, however, the American nursing terms used had been somewhat of a barrier to accurate collection of data in the UK, where different terminology applies to similar interventions. So with permission, the terms had been anglicized and adopted for use as statistical returns in an English context. Parish Nursing Ministries UK had been collecting these statistics annually since 2007.

A closer look at the sixty-eight categories offered by that tool revealed that although they related to a range of possible interventions by a parish nurse, they also encompassed a broad range of missional activities that could be undertaken by a congregation, with or without a parish nurse. Furthermore, these interventions reflected the kind of activities that might flow from a wholistic understanding of both Old and New Testaments. For

7. Livability, *Church Health Check*.

8. Johnson et al., "Documenting the Practice," 241.

example, bereavement care derives from the Biblical instruction to care for widows and orphans;[9] and forgiveness facilitation is based on Jesus' command to forgive those who sin against us.[10] The offer of first aid training would seem to be an appropriate intervention if church members are to be offered tools for caring for those who are different from them and in immediate physical need, as exemplified in the parable of the Good Samaritan.[11] The need for exercise promotion and nutritional counseling are drawn from the concept of caring for the physical body, about which Paul writes in his letter to the Corinthians. He suggests that for the believer the body is the temple of the Holy Spirit.[12] That being the case, there is also a future implication for those who are not yet believers but may become so. The assessment of a church's involvement in mission might therefore include all these interventions.

Should this study only look at those actions which are done with people who do not own faith for themselves? It was felt that this would be difficult to explore because it would necessitate intimate knowledge of a person's spiritual state, which is a condition known only to that person and God. Furthermore, there would seem to be some missional legitimacy for working with believers; Paul reminds Timothy of the need to endure hardship and to focus on the task in hand, as a soldier. Soldiers know that physical and mental fitness will help them to do this.[13] It follows that church members should keep as fit as they can, if they are remain able to continue their work in the Kingdom of God. Consequently, a church's mission activity may encompass many kinds of intervention both with those who confess Jesus Christ as Lord and those who do not.

This table of sixty-eight possible interventions therefore seemed a comprehensive way of enabling ministers to name the kind of mission action with which their church was engaged, and so was used as part of the questionnaire. Should the minister have wanted to record a category that was not offered in the sixty-eight, space was made available for additional ones to be written in.

But the inclusion of so many different interventions in this study brought another issue to the fore: church members are often to be found

9. James 1:27.
10. Matt 6:14.
11. Luke 10:25–37.
12. 1 Cor 3:16.
13. 2 Tim 2:3–6.

engaging in these actions in their homes or places of work as part of their everyday lives, voluntary work for other bodies or paid carers. Paul's instructions to the young church in Colossae are relevant here: "And whatever you do, whether in word or deed, do it all in the name of the Lord Jesus, giving thanks to God the Father through Him."[14] Whilst this is to be expected, deeply desirable, and likely to emanate from their Christian understanding of service to the community, it was not always done as an action on behalf of the local church or even publicly acknowledged as being done in the name of Christ. Parish nursing, like church-run toddler groups, or Alpha courses, or other church-based outreach events, is very clearly done on behalf of the local church, and in the name of Christ. All parish nurses produce leaflets for their clients that state this. It was therefore important that in determining the difference that a parish nurse makes to the mission of a local church, comparisons were made with other action that was taken in the name of the church. The concept of "church time" was introduced in order to facilitate such comparison. "Church time" was the amount of time spent by either the paid staff or by volunteers during which they were engaged in activities that were clearly owned by the local church, or done openly in the name of Christ by the local church.

Columns were offered alongside these interventions—one for the minister's action, one for congregational action, and one for parish nurse action in the sample where a parish nurse was attached to the church. Furthermore, the categories listed could be later grouped into different forms of wholistic mission promoting physical, mental, social and spiritual health. That gave the potential for this tool to be used to assess the range of different interventions offered by a church and the extent to which they covered all four aspects of a whole-person, Biblically-sourced, definition of health.

A consequence of using this tool for the research was that it could be and was in fact later developed as a mission audit tool for any church. It gave a picture of the kinds of mission interventions the church was engaged in, and a perspective on those aspects of whole-person mission that were not being addressed by them.

Further questions were devised relating to the context of the church, attendance at weekly worship events, ethnicity, community match, age-range of attendees, church mission statement, time spent working with people who were not regular worship attendees, and any health professionals who

14. Col 3:17.

were part of the congregation.[15] It was decided not to ask a question about theological stance, because of the varieties of interpretation around the various terms that might be offered; the word "evangelical," for example, can be understood as denoting a church that spends much time knocking on neighborhood doors with the distribution of tracts. It can also be used to differentiate a more socially active but gospel-orientated church from one with a strongly "liberal" theology. It was felt that these variables in perception of the terminology would render the classification of church by theological stance somewhat unreliable.

This design of questionnaire was then tested with colleagues and found to be an effective tool. But there was still some clarification needed about the concept of "church time" and what is done in the community in the name of the local church. The difficulty related to question seven: "Do you and/or your church volunteers spend time working with people who are not regular Sunday worship attendees, on behalf of the church? If so, please circle the percentage of church time spent in this way."

These seemed to be questions rarely asked of ministers or congregations, and therefore required some careful thought. Yet they were important for the study because it had been established that part of the mission of a local church is the level and content of its corporate engagement with people who do not attend. As already discussed, engagement may happen in individual ways, for example through paid employment, or working in the name of another voluntary organization. But as discussed above, this research is focused upon that which is publicly known as happening on behalf of the local church. Like teachers, bankers, and bus drivers, in any one week the nurse will also do individual work in a way that glorifies God in other contexts but for that she or he will not be working in the name of the local church and may not even be allowed to acknowledge Christ openly. However, when she or he works as a parish nurse, those hours are clearly worked in the name of the local church. A further query related to sheet B: "Please tick which of these activities you or other members of the congregation have been involved in as part of the church's mission within the last eighteen months."

These clarifications were addressed by using the word "outreach" instead of "mission," which seemed to improve understanding of the phrase.

---

15. See Appendix 2

## The Statistical Returns

The same statistical return had been used for all UK Parish nurses over several years and so many of them were now used to keeping appropriate records and filling it in. Not all nurses would submit returns, and since PNMUK does not employ them, it cannot insist on this. However, in completing them, there is a benefit for the church and any local grant-making bodies in that they also get a statistical view of what their parish nurse is doing with his or her church time. Use of these statistics as a tool to answer the research question would not have been sufficient; the nurses all worked different numbers of hours, had diverse expertise in dealing with different age-groups, and the ministers' perspectives would not have been collected. But between twenty and forty forms have been returned each year and so it was possible to gain an average picture of parish nurse work through these. They served to augment the primary tools and helped to compose a more comprehensive picture of parish nurse work over a longer period of time.

## The Interviews

The open-ended questions used for semi-structured interviews were designed to elicit stories and provide further information. They were structured so that the transcripts would follow a similar pattern, thus making it easier to detect any common themes.[16] Again, these questions were tested with colleagues before being finalized. A key factor was to find out whether the way they were worded would produce the kind of information that was needed to answer the research question. The questions for nurses were similar to those for ministers.

It was decided to record and analyze the conversations, looking for any indications of change in missional activity brought about by the parish nurse ministry. The recordings would be transcribed by the researcher and returned to the interviewee to check for accuracy. This was an important technique that would ensure that there were no unintended mistakes recorded or false implications in the way any sentence might be understood.[17] Interviews would be held in private so that the interviewee did not feel inhibited by the presence of others. The interviewer would be the same person every time to ensure consistency and would conduct the interview

16. See Appendices 3, 4.

17. Depoy and Gitling, *Introduction to Research*, 230.

at a location of the interviewee's choice, to assist with a relaxed informal approach.

## Ethical Considerations

The ethical guidelines for research as published by the University of Wales at the time of beginning the research were followed.[18] None of the ministers were under twenty-one or in the category of vulnerable adult, so no special precautions were necessary in this regard. However, in order to promote good research practice, stay within the code of practice of the Nursing and Midwifery Council, and work within University ethical guidelines, it was important to ensure confidentiality. This was achieved by arranging a one-to-one meeting with no others in hearing; by keeping the records of interviews in a secure place; and by changing the names of any clients mentioned. In addition, the interviews were written up with the name of the minister and nurse numbered so that no one apart from the researcher could identify the church or the location of practice.

Each person interviewed was given the option of not being recorded; they were assured of the confidentiality procedures, and they were given the option of not answering a question if they preferred not to do so.

### PROCEDURES

The research was begun with the parish nurse churches. The questionnaire was then offered to Baptist churches without parish nurses, in order to assess its use as a general mission evaluation tool, and finally extended to Baptist, Anglican, and Evangelical churches in order to establish a control group for the parish nurse study.

## The Parish Nurse Churches

The introductory letter along with the pre-interview survey was sent to all twenty-nine churches.[19] Given the pressures on the time of a minister, it

---

18. It should be noted that the university's ethical guidelines have since changed and it is likely that any repeat of this research would need to be approved by an ethics committee.

19. See Appendix 1.

was surprising to receive back fifteen positive responses, all with completed pre-interview surveys. All interviews were conducted by the researcher, recorded with a microphone and minidisc player, and later transcribed by the researcher. The transcriptions were sent back by email to the interviewee in every case for checking and they were also invited to add comments if they wished. Most interviewees did not wish to comment but a few made minor corrections to enable the spoken narrative to flow more smoothly in written form.

Reflexivity became an important factor in the conduct of the interviews, as the researcher tried conscientiously to ensure that she led from one question to another without giving signs of approval or disapproval of the answers given. Four of the interviews were conducted and recorded by telephone due to the researcher's temporary medical inability to travel. Concern was felt that these interviews would not be so productive, and if the subjects had been unknown to the interviewer, that may have been the case; but all four interviewees were nurses or ministers personally known, and a telephone did not seem to inhibit conversation. Two of the interviews, where the first recording had been incomplete, were later repeated in full and recorded by telephone, with the same questions. Interviews at one church were recorded through note-taking because one interviewee was not comfortable with recording.

## The Churches without Parish Nurses

The three-page survey that had been filled in prior to the interviews was then reduced to a two-page survey by omitting those questions that related specifically to the parish nurses. This was offered to a wider sample of churches to see if the model of interventions that had used for the parish nurse churches could also be relevant for churches without a parish nurse. This wider sample consisted of all those Baptist churches within the researcher's area of responsibility that responded to an invitation to fill in the questionnaire. Invitations were sent to eighty ministers and thirty-eight of them responded. These ministers were from a wide variety of churches in urban, suburban and rural contexts, and memberships ranging from sixteen to three hundred and forty. The results from these churches showed that the range of missional interventions they engaged with in the previous eighteen months also varied widely. For example, one small rural church was engaged in the same comprehensive range of interventions as two of the largest churches in urban areas. For some churches there was very little involvement with mental, physical, or community health issues, most of their church time being taken up with spiritual interventions. For others, whilst their building was used for mental, physical, or community activities, this was not done on behalf of the church, nor were church members involved in those activities; they were simply landlords renting out rooms. They therefore recorded a very small range of interventions.

Physical health interventions featured in most of the results but mental, community, and spiritual interventions were more frequently ticked. Ministers appreciated this tool as an additional way to evaluate the breadth of their church's engagement in mission. It may be helpful as an extra resource for those attempting mission enabling work in future.

This exercise gave the researcher confidence to offer the survey to an even wider sample of churches without parish nurses, in a random opportunistic way. It was done through the willingness of diocesan and regional representatives to circulate the questionnaires. They were also replicated on "survey-monkey," an internet-based means of gathering data. Emails were sent to Baptist, Anglican, and Evangelical ministers, through contacts in regional ministry, offering them the link to this survey. This yielded a further thirty-nine responses making seventy-seven returned questionnaires from non-parish nurse churches in total.

The majority of data was collected within the period July 2008 to December 2009. Four remaining interviews were conducted in 2010 and the two incomplete recordings were repeated in April 2011.

## DATA ANALYSIS

Each returned survey was entered in an excel database so that the raw data could be sorted. An attempt was made to group the interventions into separate sections; physical, mental, social and spiritual.[20] This was not easy to do, since many of the interventions spanned more than one group. Some of the categories, for example, an Alzheimer carers' support group, might have been placed in the social section by one researcher and in the mental health section by an alternative researcher. It was important to remember here as elsewhere in the study that "the researcher's self is inevitably an integral part of the analysis."[21] However this classification did give some guidance

20. Appendix 5.
21. Denscombe, *Good Research Guide*, 268.

as to the range of interventions offered by a church, and therefore to the expression of the concept of wholeness in its mission activity.

The churches were classified according to size and context. The same procedure was adopted with the seventy-seven churches that did not have a parish nurse.

The interview transcripts from the nurses were compared and searched for any comments that relate to personal vocation. All the transcripts were then examined for any comments relating to the five missional criteria outlined at the end of chapter 3 and their corresponding nine questions. Simple statements had been devised for each of these nine questions and as shown in chapter 5, fig.5. Any comments relating to each statement could then be collated in lists, one list for ministers' responses and one for parish nurses' responses. Different colors were used for each church to enable easy identification.

The annual statistics from PNMUK for 2010 were averaged and used as additional supporting evidence of the kind of interventions that were most commonly recorded by the nurses.

## TRUSTWORTHINESS

The reliability of all these methods depended upon the truthful responses of the participants as they understand both the questions and the interventions they were making at the time of responding to the research. This was validated to some extent by using more than one method to answer the research question and by interviewing minister and nurse separately. The transcripts of the responses in the interviews were also checked by the respondents at a later date, by which time they may have thought of other responses that could be made. In the event, very few people changed any of their transcripts, and those that did, only changed things that made for better English.

The questionnaires received from churches without parish nurses were all filled in by ministers or vicars. This was felt to give some parity with the pre-interview surveys, also filled by ministers or vicars.

## LIMITATIONS OF THIS METHODOLOGY

At the time of inviting participation, there were only twenty-nine churches that had experienced parish nursing for a minimum of eighteen months, and this reflected the fact that it was then still early days for parish nursing in the UK. However, the numbers have been increasing every year and so the reliability of this research might be improved by repeating the exercise with a larger sample of churches with parish nurses. That would introduce the problem of having to choose which respondents to interview and a different tool might need to be utilized in order to ensure that bias was not present.

The methodology selected measured breadth of activity more than outcomes and range of interventions rather than time spent on any one intervention. Some churches may have focused a great deal of their energy and time on one or two types of intervention. If they did that, this methodology would not reveal the extent of that activity. But the reason for the focus on the range of interventions rather than the time spent on any one of them was the need to look at the degree to which the church is engaged in truly wholistic mission. A different methodology would have been needed if time spent on any one intervention were to be measured.

The questionnaire examined activities and outputs rather than outcomes. Where grant funding is to be sought from charitable organizations or statutory bodies, churches will also need to develop ways of demonstrating outcomes. But as has been shown in chapter three, a Biblical assessment of mission is more closely concerned with what the church does rather than how people respond, and toward this purpose the tools used were likely to suffice.

The interviews themselves were all conducted by the researcher, which meant that there was consistency in the way the questions were asked and the same open-ended questions were used for all interviews. However, because the researcher had an interest in the outcome of the research, interviewees may have selected evidence that they thought she might want to hear, and omitted other important facts. The only way to overcome this would have been to employ an objective researcher but finance did not allow for this.

The sample of churches without a parish nurse that completed the survey had a denominational bias towards Baptists. This was simply because of a tendency among many ministers to complete surveys only if they know the researcher and wish to assist with the research. Efforts made to reach more Anglican priests did not yield so many responses. This sample of churches without a parish nurse also included some rural churches with less than fifty regular attendees. Although some of the parish nurse churches were rural they all had at least fifty attendees. This imbalance was thought to be significant and so the comparisons were made a second time, leaving the small churches out of the control group.

The annual statistical returns available through Parish Nursing Ministries UK have only been used as a partial source of information in this research, for the reasons given earlier. However, they are worthy of inclusion as a means of triangulation, because they used the same model for defining interventions and they provided a broader canvas upon which the research can be viewed.

# 5

# Findings Relating
# to the Fifteen Parish Nurse Churches

THERE WERE FIVE SOURCES of information that provided helpful insights in response to the research question. The first three related to the fifteen churches with parish nurses: the pre-interview written surveys completed by ministers; the interview transcripts with ministers of churches that had a parish nurse; and the interview transcripts with their parish nurses.

The fourth source was the annual statistical analysis for 2010 from a wider group of thirty-four parish nurses. Information from these four sources will be reported in this chapter.

A fifth source of material was a control study in the form of written surveys from a random sample of seventy-seven ministers without a parish nurse. This will be presented in chapter 6.

The two sets of interview transcripts gave the most comprehensive information. The interviewer was aware that she was likely to influence the interviewees by her interest in the subject and so made a conscious attempt not to use tone of voice or non-verbal communication to indicate the response she might be expecting. The questions had been devised in an open-ended way, so that the wording of the question did not give the inter-viewee any direction as to what the desired answers might be. In the event the interviewee conversation flowed freely and in an uninhibited way, the researcher rarely having to say much more than the questions as written. These transcripts have offered the primary evidence, and the pre-interview surveys have contributed to it. The annual statistics for 2010 have been added where they offer a perspective with information from a wider sample of parish nurse projects.

Since the five missional criteria outlined in chapter 3 formed the framework for deciding the extent to which the appointment of a parish nurse makes a difference to the mission of the local church, it was decided to use these as the pattern for writing up the results. In chapter 4, nine statements were derived from these five criteria and these form the topics around which the findings are grouped. It is worth repeating these in the table below to clarify the framework within which the results are reported. Any additional findings that that were helpful to the study in subsidiary ways are described towards the end of this chapter.

| Table 1: A framework for the writing up of the research | |
|---|---|
| Missional criteria | Relating statements that have been used to classify the responses |
| a. The release and deployment of all members who experience a sense of God's call to ministries of various kinds. | 1. Our parish nurse recruits/trains/coordinates/supports volunteers. |
| b. Involvement in activities that promote physical, mental, social and spiritual health. | 2. Our parish nurse promotes physical health. 3. Our parish nurse promotes mental health. 4. Our parish nurse promotes healthy community interaction. 5. Our parish nurse is involved in activities that promote spiritual health. |
| c. The extension of God's reign, and the offer of his salvation amongst people that do not yet know Him. | 6. Our parish nurse works with people who do not normally come to church. 7. Our parish nurse helps people find God's offer of salvation. |
| d. Respect for the God-given gift of free will that offers choices to people of all backgrounds and faiths. | 8. Our parish nurse works with people in a way that respects free will and choice. |

| e. The integration of evangelism and social engagement in such a way that both engaging with the world's needs and proclaiming the word of God are part of the same task. | 9. Our parish nurse integrates discussions about faith and prayer with her health interventions. |
|---|---|

## DOES THE PARISH NURSE RECRUIT/TRAIN/ COORDINATE/SUPPORT VOLUNTEERS?

Most of the parish nurses interviewed were volunteers themselves, working for the church on a sessional, expenses only basis. Three of them worked some paid hours for their churches, but all of these also did voluntary hours.

Eleven of the fifteen ministers interviewed specifically mentioned volunteers around the parish nurse. Of the four who did not refer to other volunteers at all, their nurses did.

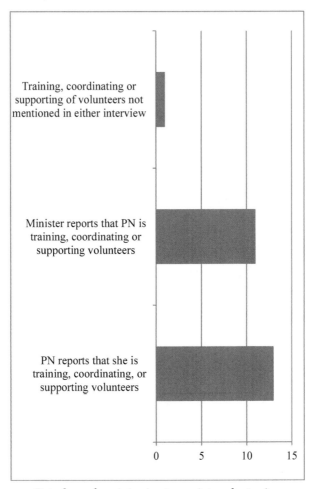

**Data drawn from interview transcripts: volunteering**

Some of the comments related to recruitment, some to training, and some to support or coordination of existing volunteers, so the results are divided into three categories: recruitment, training/coordination and support.

## Recruitment of Volunteers

The recruitment of volunteers was not a direct question in the semi-structured interviews, because of the need to be careful not to frame a closed question with an obvious positive answer, but it was hoped that an open-ended question about ways in which the parish nurse had interacted with people who were regular church attendees, would elicit responses relevant to this topic. Six of the fifteen ministers and nine of the fifteen nurses specifically mentioned recruitment of volunteers in their interviews. One minister commented that there were now volunteers that he had not been able to recruit without her.

> M2: I think I would probably find, without the parish nurse, that there would be a number of things I'd want to do which I just wouldn't even begin to start attempting, and actually trying to get volunteers and core people around to make things happen, it's not easy. There's childcare involved in the activities. Baby and toddler group, she gets three or four people running that each week. I forgot to mention Sunday crèche, we didn't have a crèche before and she got some people doing that. We do get an increasing number of kids on Sundays and she gets some of the mothers on a rota basis, so yes, she does involve people.

Another said:

> M6: That's when we brought in the health and faith care team, of about eight or ten people I think. Only in that we've got this team together. Yes absolutely, she's got this team of 8-9 people, and she does inspire them, they want to come on board, we've got a paramedic, we've got an orthopedic guy, we've got a lady who does feet, a Macmillan nurse, and she just gets them all on board, and we do promotions, and when we do promotions at church events they're all on board with her, there's a good volunteer team, and then people come and help them, so yes, very much so.

And another:

> M11: Yes I just think one thing I perhaps didn't mention earlier that has been a particular blessing to us is that the parish nurse went to speak to our young adults group because we're trying to get teams together serving folk in different ways, and she went to speak to our younger folk about this, and they've got a particular name they're called "Safari," so they set up something called "Safari Ground force," and they set themselves up to help anyone in the community who needed practical help with gardening, decorating, etc. and they've been well used, not just with contacts generated by the parish nurse, but with contacts found through the church both in helping folk in need in the church and beyond

as well. So I would say it's what the parish nurse can inspire as well as what the parish nurse can do that's been important for us.

PN14 said that she had now recruited twenty-five volunteers. And three parish nurses—PN4, PN8, and PN13—specifically spoke of recruiting volunteers that were not church people.

In the pre-interview surveys of the fifteen ministers, twelve agreed with the statement that the number of people volunteering for activities had increased since the appointment of the Parish nurse, and five of these were in strong agreement with that statement. One (M5) declined to answer that question, and two (M3 and M10) disagreed with the statement. M3 later explained that this was because they already had a culture of volunteering in their church and there was no shortage of volunteers. PN10 mentioned five volunteers in her interview.

In the annual statistics for 2010, when thirty-four nurses from thirty-one churches submitted returns, the average number of volunteers per nurse was 17.3.

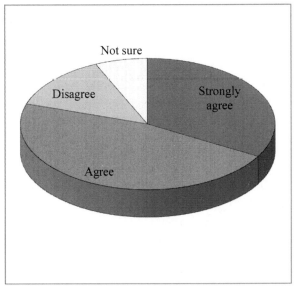

Ministers pre-interview question C2: the number of people volunteering has increased

## Training/Coordination of Volunteers

Three ministers specifically mentioned that the parish nurse had been involved in training volunteers, and six ministers also spoke of coordination of volunteers. Five parish nurses described instances of training or coordination. One minister reported plans for a befriending scheme for elderly people for which the parish nurse would do assessments and be involved in training the volunteers. Another minister described a major weekly volunteer-run event that the parish nurse had initiated and continued to coordinate:

> M1: She's been very involved in the community . . . she's set up a drop-in centre, ecumenically run, one day a week, in one of the churches in the town, very well attended, with lots of volunteers.

One nurse reported how volunteers that she had originally recruited and trained were now going on to other spheres of service:

> PN6: It started off at first that the volunteers were very very involved. We were told we had to have a good support team and they were. That has changed . . . they've grown themselves and started developing their own ministries alongside parish nursing, in the environment etc. a few of them have found out that they love doing certain aspects and they've diversified really. So I don't still have them as great helpers, one has gone off to do a counseling course, which is something she actually does quite well, she just knows she's supposed to be doing it. Another one's become an environmentalist, so we've not had as many meetings this year. At first I thought well maybe the team's not working, but actually the team has changed. Our needs have changed. I don't have the need of the support team so much but I know who I'll ask to do things, and I'll know they are always available.

In the pre-interview surveys completed by ministers, category B62 related to volunteer coordination. Eleven of the fifteen ministers named the parish nurse as involved in volunteer coordination. And twelve of the fifteen churches, 80 percent, were involved in this activity.

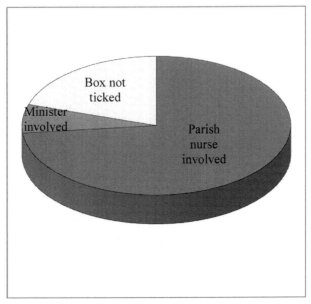

**Ministers pre-interview question B62: parish nurse involvement in volunteer coordination**

In the annual statistical returns for 2010, nurses were asked if they had conducted or organized any training sessions for the volunteers involved in the project, and if so, how many of such sessions had taken place in the year. Some nurses had organized more than one session, but most had offered at least one such session in 2010.

## Support of volunteers

One minister highlighted the parish nurse's role in supporting a volunteer:

> M1: There's someone who is married to one of our key individuals, and they are always helping everyone else. She is one of the parish nurse's volunteers. She has her own needs but has not been able to share them with anyone until the parish nurse came alongside and gained her confidence . . . She is able to continue volunteering and is supported by the parish nurse in this.

Another spoke of the way that the parish nurse was able to be a resource for existing volunteers:

M5: I think they've now learnt to go to the parish nurse if they've got someone who's got a particular issue, they think they're out of their depth and they will go to her.

A parish nurse reported how the health promotional activities she had initiated had resulted in the church family supporting each other more:

PN11: The breakfasts have been brilliant, they're such good fun apart from anything else, and it's been a way of getting the church family together in a very informal way, so they're building relationships with each other and supporting each other more.

In the pre-interview surveys completed by ministers, category B63 related to volunteer support. Ten of the fifteen ministers named her as involved in support of volunteers. And fourteen of the fifteen churches, 93 percent, of the parish nurse churches were engaged in this activity.

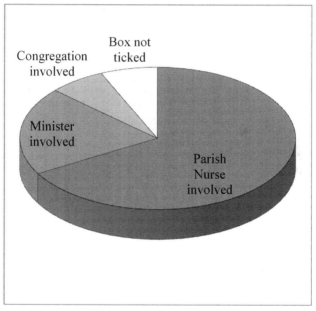

**Ministers pre-interview survey B63: parish nurse involvement in volunteer support**

Clearly, the parish nurses are engaged with volunteers. Some of them may be people who would have been volunteering in other capacities if the parish nurse had not been there, but the volunteers included in the statistical returns are those who are specifically supporting parish nurse activities. The majority of ministers in the parish nurse churches agree that the number of people volunteering has increased. Where the interview responses referred to volunteers, they indicate that the parish nurse has opened up further opportunities for volunteering in the areas of hospitality, administration, caring, listening, praying, support of health education events, facilitation of support groups and practical help for families with health needs. Training for volunteers is offered by most nurses and some have well-organized coordination arrangements.

## DOES THE PARISH NURSE ENGAGE IN PHYSICAL HEALTH INTERVENTIONS?

Not surprisingly, all of the fifteen ministers and all of the fifteen parish nurses gave accounts of instances where physical health interventions were part of the parish nurse activities. One minister described how this was done in partnership with the Primary Care Trust:

> M3: Exercise promotion . . . we ended up getting a lot of leaflets from our Primary Care trust, which we circulated and in terms of healthy eating, she went into our tots and toddler groups in terms of promoting good practice for child care and just getting alongside the mums and dads and if they had questions, taking those things in as well. The PCT then started running a keep fit class for the over 50s in the church, two sessions on a Tuesday morning. They hire the building from us, people pay them for coming, but our PN works alongside the organizer of that in terms of promoting things to do with church and we ran something called "Coffee Craft" on the back of that. They could do exercise but then stay for coffee, cake and craft.

Clinics run from church buildings are a common theme:

> M14: A number of different things, but the major one as far as the church is concerned is the surgery on a Friday morning which is a couple of hours which is open to the whole community, not just our own, but people from outside as well. That deals with blood-pressures, blood sugars, etc but also majors on people's health concerns and anxieties. People are anxious about something they don't want to trouble a doctor or they can't always get to a doctor so popping into the surgery they're reassured; the parish nurse will do checks and because she has contact with both surgeries, she can refer people on or suggest they visit a doctor. That's obviously a big step forward. We also do a mini surgery once a fortnight in the

local luncheon club, where they get about 80 people and about ten of them queue up to see the PN about all sorts of different things. So they don't have to come to church, we're taking it out into the community as well. She also visits the care home and works with the residents there on fitness, but also does health checks, and builds up trust, which is a lot of what this is about.

Sometimes the physical health work extended to neighboring churches:

> M10: She's made links with the Methodist church and she's begun to do a clinic there as well She's done a lot on diabetes so that she knows quite a lot about that and I think she's been asked about different other aspects of health from time to time.

Another minister cited the work done with physical health for men:

> M9: The men's health checks . . . that type of thing has worked very well, I think people received that very well. Because it's a very easy entry level to come in, to be discussing health issues with somebody, without thinking you've got to make an appointment. A lot of the health services locally, a lot of the agencies locally have expressed a great appreciation for what she's done.

The parish nurses elaborated further on this topic: one used the taking of blood pressure as a way to encourage people to talk about other health matters, be they physical, mental or spiritual. She also used notice-boards and tables to get information about physical health across to congregation members and hall users.

> PN6: I have a blood pressure session after every service, where one of my team does blood pressures or I do them, and one of my team is available, or I'm available or talk. I have notice-boards for the church hall users; I have a table at the back of church that has different health promotions and health issues on, which is changed on a very regular basis, depending on what health topic I'm looking at, at any one time, or what comes up in the media or within the church. Any social function we have, we offer blood pressures. I have taken one of the new members into the toddler club that runs in our church hall . . . it's not run by the church. I did a big spread on meningitis awareness, went round talking to each mum individually. I have two notice-boards in the church hall. The hall is used by Al-anon, narcotics anonymous, Tai Chi, uniformed organizations, an art class, and just quite a few different people out

there. A dancing class, and an acting class. I have notice-boards
and leaflet dispensers and the leaflets do go.

The subjects they mentioned included the promotion of good nutri-
tion, weight management, the introduction of fruit to church catering, food
cooperatives, health walks, exercise classes, monitoring of physical care for
post-operative patients, medication management, screening, health fairs,
dying care, falls prevention, and foot-care.

The pre-interview surveys with ministers revealed that their fifteen
parish nurses were involved in all twenty-one of the physical interventions.
The most common physical health activities attributed to parish nurses
were health screening, health system guidance, health education, exercise
promotion, medication management, and nutritional counseling. With
their congregation members, approximately half of the fifteen nurses were
also said to be doing risk assessment, self care facilitation and foot care. In
total, the parish nurse churches were involved in almost 70 percent of the
possible physical interventions offered in the survey tool.

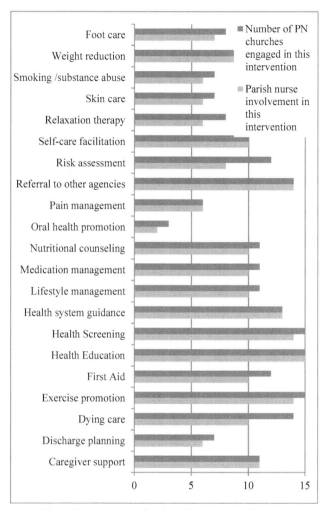

**Physical interventions by churches with parish nurses**

The annual statistics from thirty-four nurses in 2010 support this picture. They show that the most common physical health interventions were health education, health screening, and health system guidance, exercise promotion, dying care, medication management, and lifestyle management.

As might be expected, these findings all suggested that the appointment of a parish nurse has increased a church's involvement in physical health interventions. We now turn to other types of care.

## DOES THE PARISH NURSE ENGAGE IN MENTAL HEALTH INTERVENTIONS?

Parish nurses are only able to work to the competences for which they have been trained and although there are parish nurses who are trained in mental health, and work more intensively with clients who have mental health problems, they were not represented in the interview sample.

However, five ministers described supportive mental health interventions by their parish nurses:

> M3: We had recently a contact with Social Services about a schizophrenic, who asked through the links with parish nursing can someone be involved with this person, that person subsequently through discussions with them, coming to church regularly now, and actually would say that their health is improving with medication.

> M7: A chap up the road whose mother lived next door, he was in considerable distress because his mother was clearly subsiding with a form of dementia and so the PN had to talk through with him about how to care for her, how to support her, how to recognize his own needs, how to understand what was going on, and then as she very rapidly deteriorated he needed further support. I think it's affected the quality of life, for a lot of people, because they no longer see themselves as isolated.

Eight of the fifteen parish nurses also reported some interventions with mental health issues:

> PN 4: I have a background interest in grief and bereavement work. People have come and said this was never talked about before.

One nurse described how she had set up a memory clinic in the village for people with dementia and their carers. And others met people with mental health problems at their regular drop-in sessions:

> PN7: Another person has called in on Wednesdays because he's been made redundant and he doesn't know what else to do with himself, and another one is having memory problems. These are the people who came last Wednesday. (Another lady)'s had memory problems at eighty-five years old, living alone. Accidentally left the car ignition switched on. So she had a flat battery, and for her it was just the last straw. She didn't know who she could turn to, who could sort it all out for her and she came in on the Wednesday and

said "What am I going to do . . . " So it's all sorts of people from all sorts of walks of life.

In one church a psychologist came on board with the team of parish nurse volunteers and started visiting the local care home, where she began to work with those who had dementia, or were dealing with loss or bereavement. In another the parish nurse recognized the signs of postnatal depression in someone who came to the toddler group and was able to follow that through and get her treated for it.

In the pre-interview surveys, ministers reported their parish nurses to be most often involved in the following mental health interventions: active listening, anxiety management, bereavement care, coping enhancement, counseling, decision making support, and emotional support. With the exception of anxiety management, which was attributed to the parish nurse and the minister, these activities were normally done by the minister and/or congregation members as well as by the parish nurse. In total, the parish nurse churches were involved in 60 percent of the possible mental health interventions offered by the survey tool

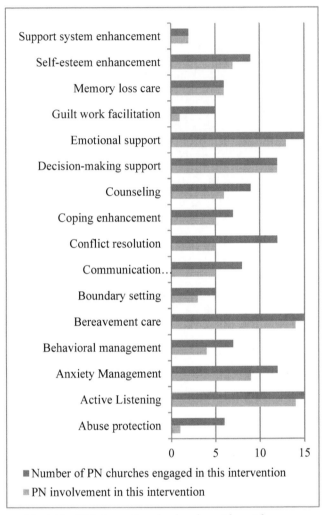

**Mental health interventions by churches with parish nurses**

In the annual statistics for 2010, active listening and emotional support featured as two of the five most common interventions offered by thirty-four nurses.

## DOES THE PARISH NURSE ENGAGE
## IN COMMUNITY HEALTH INTERVENTIONS?

Eleven of the ministers wrote that their parish nurse was involved in community development for health. In one this involved developing partnerships with other agencies to present healthy messages to anyone who would come in:

> M3: "Spring to life," which was for the community looking at whole person health care, so we had people coming to talk about health but we had stalls about various things so we had a church stall, we had a Hope 08 stall,[1] we had town chaplains, the hospital chaplaincy having a presence here, then we had broader; we had the council talking about "Go for life," which is their idea of getting everybody to be more fit and healthy; there was issues to do with school meals, education, disability, disability aids, to do with getting money off social services, that sort of thing, food, home delivery frozen food meals; we had about 30-40 stalls, we had it opened, the mayor came in. The whole emphasis was on promoting whole person health, and we had, through the day, fashion shows for charity shops. About 350 people (came) through into the building that day from the community, to come and explore what was on offer, and as a result of that then the council ran a very similar day for over 50s which we were invited to be involved in. as parish nursing and as a church. And that had thousands of people come through that as well, and as a result of that, in terms of the church being more involved in the community, the council then ran at the beginning of this year an event for spiritual carers, and what resources were available for spiritual carers. And virtually every church in town was invited to a day in a hotel and the council doing something like spring to life really, with all the resources in one place, and so its had quite a big knock on effect. There are those who've caught the vision in the council and picked up on those themes, those ideas as well. That's been received very positively.

In a multicultural area the intervention was in the field of community cohesion as described here:

> M2: After holiday at home we looked at Fridays and a lot of the people who came to holiday at home now come to a community

---

1. "Hope 08" was an ecumenical effort by churches in the UK to reach out to local communities with a message of hope.

lunch, followed by drop-in activities. And again the parish nurse is very much involved in the planning of that and making that happen. And we managed to get a Muslim artist to come and do some art work which would later be displayed down at the station. She came in and did this and we struck up a good friendship with her, and she helps us out. The parish nurse wanted to do something at half-term. We've got links with another woman who is a Hindu, and our parish nurse's concern was that so often that our young people live their religious lives in isolation and then go off to University and encounter stuff that they haven't before. She felt it's better to be aware of other faiths by allowing people to mix and explore difference, so we experimented with this thing, put up a Bedouin's tent with all sorts of cloths and things, and then we did a Christingle for the Christian festival, and there was some lamp-making for the end of Ramadan and all the energy for that came from the parish nurse.

Thirteen of the parish nurses described ways in which they assisted the development of a healthy community. One took a group outing to a crematorium to help take away some of the mystery behind what happens there. Another was involved in the commencement of a hospital to home scheme:

> PN12: We surveyed the whole of the local village community to try and establish what the needs were. We've continued to try and go down that route. To concentrate on what the needs are, rather than do things we think the community needs. That is particularly so with the new hospital to home scheme. That was the need we could see so we tried to fulfill that need.

A parish nurse in a market town saw the need for lonely people to get together and set up a drop-in centre:

> PN1: I picked up a few ideas from other parish nurses. And through that we did some occasional Sunday afternoon tea parties for people on their own. And then we started a drop-in centre manned by the church people, churches together volunteers. Probably we get 80 to 100 people in every week for coffee and lunch and the majority are not churchgoers, so that's good . . . That has been a massive challenge, to get that going, to get all the churches together, to get the Congregational church where it's being hosted, on board with it, and keeping them on board, just treading very carefully with them, that has been an enormous challenge.

The pre-interview surveys showed that thirteen of the fifteen ministers thought that their parish nurse was involved in family support; twelve cited end of life issues and networking; eleven thought their parish nurses were involved in advocacy, crisis intervention, and volunteer coordination; and ten of the fifteen ministers also mentioned volunteer support. In most of the categories, the minister, or other members of the congregation also participated in these activities. In total, the parish nurse churches were involved in 67 percent of the possible community health interventions offered by the survey tool.

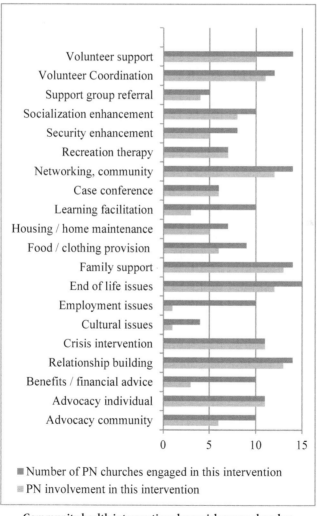

**Community health interventions by parish nurse churches**

In the annual statistics for 2010, a similar pattern appeared, with family support, community networking, volunteer coordination, and support featuring most commonly.

## DOES THE PARISH NURSE ENGAGE IN SPIRITUAL HEALTH INTERVENTIONS?

Fourteen of the fifteen ministers reported that their parish nurses engaged in some form of spiritual health care. This ranged from praying with people after a church service to praying with them during a consultation, or introducing a spiritual element into social activities:

> M1: She happens to be particularly good at visiting people in the last stages of life, and has been involved right up until the last stages. She regularly prays with people and offers them prayers to use in their own homes.

> M3: The PN was on the ministry team with her parish nurse badge on. So if at the end of the service people wanted prayer for anything the PN was available we felt it was important that the PN was part of that . . . not the leadership team but the ministry team.

> M2: She used to run a toddler church in her session. It wasn't a hugely successful thing, we might have had about ten adults and four to five children, but you know the kids played out here, and she did a toddler churchy thing.

One reported that the PN had helped people deal with theological questions about healing:

> M4: And she has also been running a "Living with severe illness" support group once a month for a year or two; where medication and prayers for healing haven't worked.

All fifteen parish nurses referred to the offering of spiritual care in one form or another. This ranged from offering prayer for people before or after the visit, talking about work-life balance, to praying with them, leading services, taking communion to people, and engaging in discussion about matters of faith with them.

> PN4: . . . that's what makes PN so great. You're free to talk about all aspects of life. With someone who is a church member we can talk about holiness and about what God asks of us. If someone is

angry about what a person has said or done, we talk about for-giveness. We can talk about challenging people yet at the same time caring for them. And what the implications of those demands are. It's very hard to cover all bases. I have a prayer ministry with people . . . there's a housebound lady who doesn't want to receive communion but does value presence and prayer. Healing services have been a regular part of my work. Sometimes the preaching or speaking raises an emotional or spiritual health issue.

One parish nurse had not received many requests for prayer, but many of the parish nurses expressed some surprise about the positive way in which spiritual care or the offer of prayer is received. For example, this was one response in answer to the question "Does Spiritual care feature in your work at all?"

PN11: Yes, but mainly in terms of just praying for people or pray-ing with them. I've not had anybody who's refused to be prayed with, which is surprising, given that some of these people are not from church at all. And even people that come to the breakfasts are very open to praying, which surprises me sometimes, and I think probably surprises all Christians, I think we have all come to the point of not talking about church, and not talking about God, because it's not politically correct any more, but it's amazing how, if you offer, and tell people you will pray for them, they're really pleased about that. So that's um . . . that's been a bit of an eye opener really.

In the pre-interview survey ministers reported that their parish nurses were active in all of the spiritual care categories except spiritual abuse pro-tection. Most of them were involved in pastoral care, prayer ministry, and presence when words are inadequate, spiritual care and support, group discussions about faith, and individual discussions about faith. In addition, nine of them were involved in healing services, and seven of them in sacra-mental ministry, for example taking communion to people, though not all traditions would allow this or expect it. In total, the parish nurses churches were involved in 80 percent of the possible spiritual health interventions offered by the survey tool.

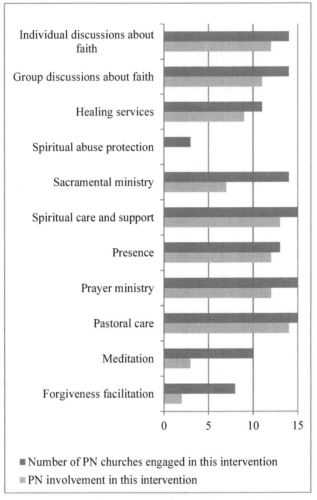

**Spiritual health interventions by parish nurse churches**

In the 2010 statistics, pastoral care, prayer ministry, and individual discussions about faith featured among the five most common interventions. Over half of the consultations included reference to faith or prayer.

## DOES THE PARISH NURSE WORK WITH PEOPLE WHO DO NOT NORMALLY ATTEND CHURCH?

In the interviews, all the ministers referred to the parish nurses engaging with people who do not normally attend church. In one case it was reported that the impact on the community has been noticed by the Chair of the

Parish Council. In another, the minister reported that the activities of the parish nurse have helped the church to gain entry into homes that would previously have been closed to them:

> M14: And it could be a practical thing, a medical thing, respite care, sitting with somebody, all sorts of different aspects which enables us to get into the community and into homes and houses that we would never even have approached the door, let alone seen it open for us to go in, and its opened up a completely new mission field for us. This has opened up doors for us to take the love and compassion of Jesus into homes and they see what's happening. It's a very important part of the mission of the church, because its just opened doors that have never ever have opened in 100 years.

All but one of the parish nurses spoke of their involvement with people who do not normally attend church, and that one, (PN10), mentioned a desire to extend the work in that way. Some of the nurses specifically mentioned people they contact through the church's weekday activities, but who do not attend services:

> PN9: We've done a lot of activities that have been more based . . . aimed at the local community . . . We've got a large group that class this as their church but they are not Christians, they just live in the local area and they use the facilities we provide, so a lot of the family facilities, the toddlers group and the playgroup. We've done a family health day which they all attended, we had 120 people through the door about 25 families within two hours, we have recently started doing messy church, so we do that at once a term and we've had anywhere up to 80/90 people come through for messy church. And all these are basically non-church families that attend for them, they're not our own church families.

In the pre-interview surveys, the ministers were asked to estimate how much church time was spent with people who did not normally come to church. Was it less than 10 percent, 10 to 25 percent, 25 to 40 percent, 40 to 55 percent, 55 to 70 percent, or more than 70 percent? The midpoint of each answer was then recorded and these figures were used to obtain an average. The ministers largely confirmed that their churches worked with people outside of the church: Six of them reported that they, the parish nurses and/ or the volunteers spent over 55 percent of church time with people who were not regular Sunday worship attendees, on behalf of the church; and four of the churches spent over 40 percent of church time in this way.

But do parish nurses themselves spend time with non-church people? Information from the 2010 annual statistics to Parish Nursing Ministries UK from thirty-four nurses may help to answer this. These showed that at least a quarter of the total personal consultations (excluding health education sessions, healing services and volunteer training) were with people who did not attend church regularly.

## DOES THE PARISH NURSE HELP PEOPLE MOVE TOWARDS A SAVING FAITH IN CHRIST?

Eleven of the fifteen ministers spoke of the way in which their parish nurse had encouraged people to take steps of faith or to attend church services or events where they might learn to do so. Here is one example of that:

> M12: There are certain people coming to church because they got involved with parish nursing. I think we've had at least 3 people coming that way. But there are other people that maybe because of her relationship with them . . . they might have been involved on the fringe of the church and came occasionally, now coming more regularly.

However, only one mentioned someone who had "come to faith" specifically as a result of the parish nurse ministry. For most, the parish nurse appeared to aid the building of relationship, the inviting to church events, or the introducing of spiritual conversation. She was seen as part of a bigger picture as suggested here:

> M4: The care that she gives is an important factor both in people coming to faith and in maintaining their faith. She's part of a whole picture, but an important part.

The parish nurses themselves gave a little more detail:

> PN5: Well what happened was, he got cancer and he decided that if he got through his chemotherapy he'd go to church. So he arrived at the church a few months ago, and we don't know how long he's got to live, he didn't think he'd make it through the chemotherapy, but he has, he's being confirmed.

> PN7: One girl has been through court proceedings re abuse. I've had to stand and hold her hand as she's been through the long drawn out process from February. I took her up to the communion rail when she came in and said "oh shall we say the Lord's prayer

together" and she didn't know the words of the Lord's prayer but she has begun to come to church regularly because of this.

One parish nurse gave her interview towards the end of the research period, and in the time that elapsed between the minister's interview and her own there appeared to be some progress on this issue:

> PN14: I've had six people actually give their lives to the Lord on a Friday, (which is when the clinic is open) through parish nursing, every single one has been through that (work), and we've got a couple of people who come to church every single week now, not made a commitment but see the need to come, and they're all through my Friday clinics.

The pre-interview surveys were the first part of the research, when some of the nurses had only just done eighteen months of their project. Questions C4, C5, and C6 related to this issue. At that time ten of the fifteen ministers agreed that they had seen spiritual growth in people who do not attend church regularly and three of these agreed strongly with that statement.

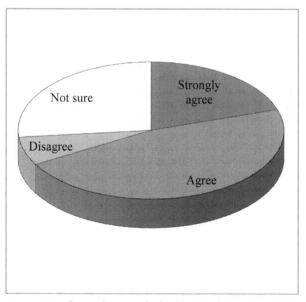

**I have seen some spiritual growth in people that the parish nurse has worked with and who do not normally attend church**

Furthermore, fourteen of the fifteen ministers agreed that they had seen spiritual growth in people who did attend church regularly, and four of these were in strong agreement.

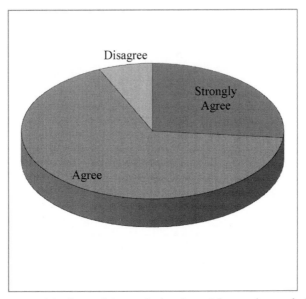

**I have seen some spiritual growth in people that the parish nurse has worked with and who normally attend church**

Question C5, was about whether or not people had come to faith partly as a result of a parish nurse intervention. There may have been different understandings of the phrase "come to faith," but there were six ministers in agreement, one of these in strong agreement, one not sure, and one abstention. The remaining seven disagreed with the statement that people had come to faith partly as a result of a parish nurse intervention.

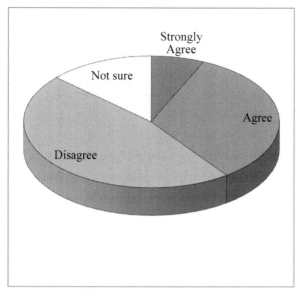

**People have come to faith, partly as a result of parish nurse interventions**

The annual statistics from thirty four nurses for 2010 do not ask whether people have come to faith, although they do show that individual discussions about faith are regularly part of a parish nurse consultation: 48 percent of parish nurse personal consultations involved discussion about faith or prayer, and 15 percent of these were with people who do not normally attend church.

Question C6 asked whether people had joined the church partly as a result of a parish nurse intervention. With hindsight, it was recognized that the meaning of the phrase "joined the church" would have been understood differently in Anglican and Baptist churches. Seven ministers agreed, with one of these in strong agreement, but eight disagreed.

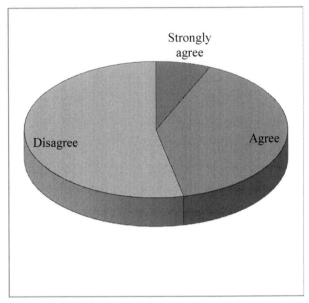

**People have joined the church, partly as a result of parish nurse interventions**

In summary, over two thirds of the ministers wrote that they had seen spiritual growth in people who do not come to church as a result of parish nurse interventions, but in more than half of the parish nurse churches this had not translated into professions of faith or new church members at the time of responding to the pre-interview survey. Nearly all of the ministers wrote that they had seen spiritual growth in church people with whom the parish nurse had worked.

## DOES THE PARISH NURSE WORK WITH PEOPLE IN A WAY THAT RESPECTS FREE WILL AND CHOICE?

This statement is extremely important for parish nursing, since registered nurses working under the Nursing and Midwifery Council rules are bound to respect the choice and free will of the client in every case, unless the nurse believes that harm may be caused to that client or others. Furthermore, parish nurses are dealing with vulnerable people, and it is important to ensure that no undue pressure is perceived by the client.

Without being asked directly about this, thirteen of the fifteen ministers referred to it. They said they had noticed the respectful way in which their parish nurses approached the area of spiritual care. Here is a comment from the minister of a church in a multicultural area:

> M2: And so for about a year now she's been running a health club for women. And the church was saying "why does it just have to be for women?", but the reason being, if you want Muslim women to come in and take veils off, we don't want blokes walking around, you know, and that's been quite interesting, people come and go with that.

Ministers confirmed that parish nursing care is open to all, regardless of whether or not they come to church.

> M7: And so the fact that the team is willing to help anyone regardless of their background or beliefs means that there's a huge appreciation of it, I think.

> M6: She took a big platter (of fruit) in last summer to the group. And they said, "But we don't come to your church. We cannot get past this, something for nothing." And it's just so well received, beautifully received, but they just can't understand why the church wants to do it. It's going to take time, that.

> M5: She has helped people not necessarily to bring them to church, but to bring them to a wholeness of healing.

Parish nurses offered similar insights as they spoke about their work. Here is a comment from a nurse in a multi-cultural area:

> PN2: Ah yes, we have a children's club, and we particularly tried to get a third Christians, a third Muslim, and a third Hindu, and we shared our, well we celebrated a meal each day from the their religions and we did a craft from each. And, so that was very good.

> PN5: I spend time with people who have been referred from the surgery. Last year I had three people who wanted to commit suicide. That was really difficult. I had huge support from the surgery, they didn't leave me with these people but it was very challenging, I must admit. And one of them was a Roman Catholic lady who said, "If I do this, I'll go to hell." And I sought various people saying, "This is a very deep held belief, it's not what I actually believe but how can I walk alongside this lady?"

> PN7: We get a lot of people who are self-referrals now . . . people who say, "Is this alright? I don't come to church, will you still help me?"

Whilst the question had not been asked directly, it was possible to examine all the transcripts for evidence of an attitude that offers freewill and choice, and figure 5:8a shows the frequency of this.

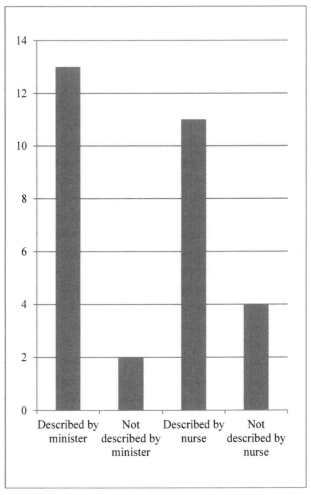

**Interview responses: working with people in a way that respects freewill and choice**

Another indicator of free will and choice would be whether or not people were being referred to other organizations and agencies. Since such referrals are only made at the client's request and/or with their willing permission, this would indicate that respect for choice of service-provider was being offered. It should be remembered however that even though they are not working for the NHS, the nurses are seen as professionals by vulnerable clients and so their choices might be influenced by that factor. In the 2010 annual statistics, thirty-four nurses made 268 referrals in the year.

Responses to one of the questions in the pre-interview survey may add to the evidence here: Question C3 asked ministers whether or not their liaison with other voluntary organizations had increased since the appointment of the parish nurse. If the answer was in the affirmative, this may suggest that clients are being referred elsewhere. Since the client needs first to agree to that referral, this could signify that choices are being offered. All ministers agreed and seven of them strongly agreed.

## DOES THE PARISH NURSE INTEGRATE SOCIAL ACTION WITH DISCUSSION ABOUT FAITH AND PRAYER?

As has been seen, the most recent emphasis in mission has been the concept of integral mission, where social action and discussion about faith and prayer belong together unless political regimes prohibit this. Yet churches often keep the two activities separate and then find themselves asking how people who access the social provision will begin to discover faith for themselves.

There were no questions in the pre-interview survey that addressed this issue, but thirteen of the fifteen ministers reflected that the integration of social action with discussions about faith was a feature of their parish nurse's work:

> M4: She does "fit for life" . . . a bridge between diet and faith. We recently had a father dying in his thirties with two young children and she provided practical help for the family along with pastoral support.

> M5: I think she manages to keep a good balance there, to help people in need when they ask for it health wise, but she's also able to link it to their spiritual life in a positive way, yes so which has helped people not necessarily to bring them to church, but to bring them to a wholeness of healing.

> M15: A lady that the parish nurse had been seeing regularly, very unwell, just being with her, praying with her, doing shopping, that kind of thing, being in touch with the family. And sadly she died, but there was a lovely letter about two weeks after the funeral from the family to say that in her last days all she would speak of is the parish nurse and what she had done for that individual.

The parish nurses echoed this:

> PN6: I try it to feature at the back of everything I'm doing. I'm trying to incorporate spiritual care. It's not always easy really, because there are topics in health where it's just not going to feature. But I always give with the spiritual care, and I try for it to be a whole part of everything I do. And obviously a lot of prayer goes in to what I try to do.

> PN12: Spiritual care has been very much part of my work . . . in that I come from the church they know that I'm coming from a spiritual background, from a Christian church. There's not always spiritual discussion, there's not always prayer, but they know, they feel relaxed enough to ask me questions. And sometimes it is possible to pray with people because you feel that it's appropriate. So yes, spiritual care does feature all the time in everything that I do . . . it has to.

> PN9: We've also had somebody who had lots and lots of treatment for being overweight and low self esteem, and had not got anywhere through other channels, doing lots of diets and things, but because we could encompass spiritual care and look deeper at what her needs were, she's actually overcome her lack of self-esteem and is well on her way to losing the weight, and she keeps telling me it's because we could look at the spiritual side of it as well as look at the physical side of things. As I accompany people to hospital appointments and things like that, it's good to be able to pray with them and to pray about their treatment and I have a particular girl with Multiple Sclerosis who I do a lot of work with and she's found it really beneficial having somebody there where she can incorporate her faith with whatever's going on.

Some commented that this was very different from their NHS work, where they reported that faith discussion and prayer was not encouraged in the context of practical care.

> PN3: I find it a lovely way to be able to share my faith. Everything that is in me as a nurse and my faith, I find it easier to share, as a Parish nurse, because of more of the restrictions when we're employed within the NHS etc., but also I think it's a tremendous opportunity for the church, a huge opportunity to get out in the community . . .

It was possible to scan all the interview transcripts for evidence of the integration of faith or prayer conversations with physical, mental or community interventions and figure 16 shows that this was verbalized by minister and/or nurse in all of the parish nurse churches.

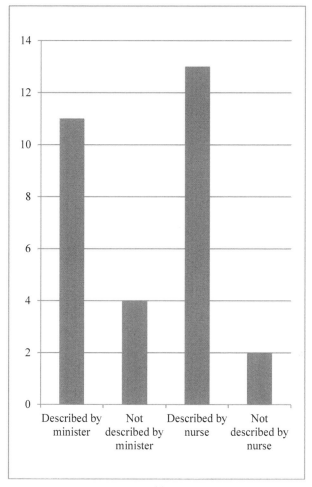

**Interview responses: integration of faith with parish nursing activities**

In the 2010 annual statistics form, it was recorded that 48 percent of the parish nurse consultations had included reference to faith or prayer.

This demonstrates two aspects of mission that a parish nurse brings to a church; first, joining faith and prayer with practical action is a natural feature of the work; and second, in keeping with the principle of choice, the offer to pray or to discuss spiritual matters is not a pre-condition of the practical action.

## OTHER RELEVANT EVIDENCE

There were several questions asked on the pre-interview survey that related to the mission of the church in general and the responses to them were helpful in answering the research question. Some of the semi-structured interview responses also touched on these more general issues.

## Ministers' Views of the Impact of a Parish Nurse on Their Mission Program

In the US, parish nurses commonly work within congregations as part of the in-house pastoral care program rather than the mission or outreach program. It was therefore important to ascertain how much UK ministers felt their parish nurse had impacted the mission program. When asked to comment on the statement that the appointment of a parish nurse had made no difference to the church's mission program all fifteen ministers disagreed and thirteen of these strongly disagreed.

Conversely, when asked if the appointment of a parish nurse had helped them to increase their mission activities, all fifteen ministers agreed, eight of them strongly.

And when asked if they would recommend other churches to appoint parish nurses in order to enhance their mission involvement, fourteen agreed, twelve of them strongly. One omitted to answer that question on the survey, but stated, "yes absolutely" to a very similar question in his interview, which may indicate it was simply an oversight.

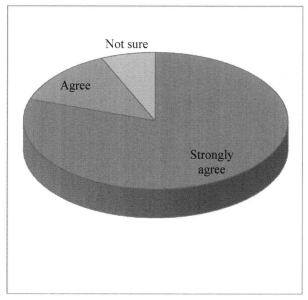

**I would recommend the appointment of a parish nurse to other churches in order to enhance their mission involvement**

In their interviews, the other ministers repeated their views on this topic. All agreed that they would recommend to other churches that they appoint a parish nurse, though some qualified this by adding thoughts such as "depending what else they are doing," or "providing they have a pastoral team in place," or "providing the minister is supportive." Four of the ministers wanted to recommend it so strongly that their tone of enthusiasm came out very clearly on the recording, and they talked about ways in which the profile of parish nursing could be raised.

## Working Relationships

In the pre-interview surveys all disagreed and thirteen of these strongly disagreed that there had been difficulties in working relationships between the parish nurse and themselves, or other church workers. No difficulties in working relationships were raised in the ministers' interviews. Furthermore, eleven of the ministers agreed that they personally or their families had received advice for health through the parish nurse, and six of these strongly agreed that they or their families had received advice for health through her.

## Nurses' Views on Their Work as Parish Nurses

All fifteen nurses were enthusiastic about their parish nursing role. Of particular significance to them was the opportunity to combine their nursing skills with the provision of immediate spiritual care, as they encountered the need, something which was not possible to achieve within the NHS. Their response to the question "Would you recommend parish nursing to other nurses" was a unanimous "yes." This extract, from one who has since moved away from the church is typical of the others:

> PN3: Oh yes definitely, definitely, I would. Yes. I would. I think the whole ethos, there are so many opportunities in the sense of sharing your faith. I find it a lovely way to be able to share my faith. Everything that is in me as a nurse and my faith, I find it easier to share, as a parish nurse, because of more of the restrictions when we're employed within the NHS etc., but also, I think it's a tremendous opportunity for the church, a huge opportunity to get out in the community; and provided you have got, . . . I know you can do it without, . . . but you need the backing of the local health service and other agencies to make it work really well. I'm not saying it wouldn't work without them, but I think it works better if you've got their support, but for me it was lovely, it was really lovely.

## SUMMARY

Information from the four sources relating to the fifteen churches with parish nurses has been presented: pre-interview written surveys completed by ministers, interview transcripts with those ministers, interview transcripts with their parish nurses, and the annual statistical analysis for 2010 from a wider group of thirty-four nurses. All of this information has been sifted and synthesized and offered by using a framework of nine questions derived from the five missional criteria identified in chapter 3. In that way it is possible to assess the degree to which the appointment of a parish nurse has made a difference to the mission of these fifteen English churches. The significance of these results will be discussed in chapter 7. However, in order to ascertain the extent to which they might have implications for other churches, the information from the control sample was placed alongside the work that was done on the parish nurse churches, and this is presented in the next chapter.

# 6

# Comparisons with the Control Group

THE RESULTS SHOWN IN chapter 5 relate to those churches that had had parish nurses for at least eighteen months at the beginning of the study period. In order to measure any difference that the appointment of a parish nurse has made to the mission of churches it was necessary to find a control group. Perhaps the most appropriate comparison would have been a similar study of those churches before they appointed the nurse, but this research began subsequent to those appointments. As explained in chapter four, it was therefore decided to use the same questionnaire as had been used for the ministers' pre-interview survey on a larger number of churches without a parish nurse, with the omission of the questions on page three, which were specifically about the parish nurse. This was an opportunistic sample of churches and the surveys were completed either on-line or on paper. It offered the possibility of examining the range of mission interventions with which churches were currently engaged.

## THE CONTROL SAMPLE

The survey was completed by seventy-seven ministers, of whom forty-four were Baptist, twenty-four were Anglican, seven were in Local Ecumenical Partnerships, one was Methodist, and one, Independent Evangelical. The corresponding denominational affiliation in the parish nurse sample was seven Baptist, seven Anglican and one Independent Evangelical. The contexts of the control group churches were: twenty rural, twenty market-town, twenty-four suburban commuter, six urban, six council housing, and one in a new-build area. The corresponding contexts for the Parish nurse churches were as follows: Six rural, two urban, two suburban commuter, two council housing, and three market town. The control group was therefore denominationally representative but weighted towards Baptist churches and contextually representative but slightly weighted towards suburban commuter churches.

Two of the seventy-seven ministers commented that they found the survey took a little too long to fill in, but all completed it.

They were varying sizes of congregations in the control sample: Twenty were small, at less than fifty attendees, twenty-eight were medium, (fifty to one hundred attendees) and twenty-nine had over one hundred regular attendees. In the parish nurse sample, none were less than fifty attendees, eight were medium sized, and seven were over one hundred attendees. There was therefore an imbalance in the control sample relating to size of congregation, but if the smaller churches had been taken out, this would also have decreased the number of rural churches in comparison to the parish nurse sample.

Thirteen of the control group churches and two of the parish nurse churches had mixed ethnic minority congregations. The rest had majority white congregations. Ten of the comparative churches and three of the parish nurse churches had female ministers, the rest were male.

In the comparative sample, 20 percent of the total attendees in the comparative sample were under twenty-one years old: 16 percent were between twenty-one and forty years old: exactly the same percentages for these ages were recorded in the parish nurse churches. But the largest age-band in the control group churches were between forty-one and sixty years old, at 29 percent, closely followed by those between sixty-one and eighty years old, at 27 percent. The congregations in the parish nurse churches were slightly older in that there were less in the age-range of forty-one to sixty (23 percent), and more in the over sixties category, (31 percent). The smallest group were the over eighties, at 7 percent and 9 percent respectively.

In the control group, then, there was an imbalance towards Baptist churches regarding denomination, a slight imbalance towards suburban commuter land regarding context, and a slight imbalance towards small churches regarding size of congregation. But considering that this was a random, self-selected group, it seemed that the comparative sample was a reasonably similar mix of churches to the ones that had been the subject of the study.

So how were these non-parish nurse churches involved in mission? And how did that compare with the parish nurse churches?

There was not as much evidence from this sample as from the parish nurse churches, because these ministers were not interviewed, and they did not compile annual statistics for 2010. Results for the criteria of "free will and choice" and "integration of evangelism and social engagement" were consequently not available. But the comparative results concerning the first three of our five missional criteria gave some useful information.

## SUPPORT OF VOLUNTEERS

The seventy-seven churches were all likely to have volunteers working in some task or other, even if the numbers were limited. However, in the survey, just 40 percent of their ministers said that they or one of their congregation members spent time coordinating volunteers; and 44 percent said they or their congregation members spent time supporting volunteers. This compares with 80 percent and 93 percent for the same questions from the ministers of parish nurse churches.

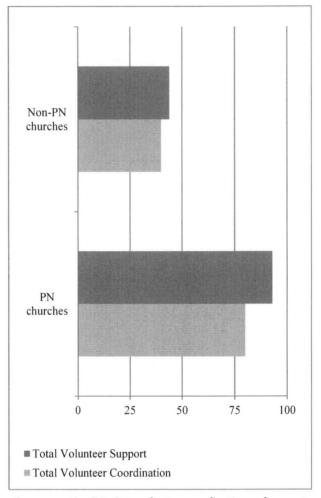

**Survey question B62, B63: volunteer coordination and support**

All parish nurses are trained to offer volunteer coordination and support and policies relating to volunteering are offered by Parish Nursing Ministries UK. It might be expected therefore that the appointment of a parish nurse has some effect in ensuring that there is volunteer coordination and support in church life. It has already been noted that the average number of volunteers working around a parish nurse is seventeen per year. Could these results suggest that more people get more involved in volunteering as a result of the appointment? A further question is whether or not these people would have been doing other voluntary work if the parish nurse had not been appointed? And, would they perhaps have come forward in a similar manner if the appointment had been say, a youth worker, or a family worker? The answer to that was not to be found in this study. However, what could be asserted is that volunteers do appear to come forward to work with a parish nurse.

The first of our criteria in looking at the mission of a local church was the release and deployment of all members who experience a sense of God's call to ministries of various kinds. It was noted in chapter 3 that God's call comes to all kinds of people for all kinds of work in his kingdom. Fifty-nine of the seventy-seven churches had health professionals as regular attendees at their church. Like the parish nurses who express a sense of call in their application for training, many of these health professionals would also see their work as a calling, even if it is in paid employment in the context of a secular health service. Most ministers said they did not have specific support structures in place for these health professionals.

Parish nurses do not work alone. They also encourage church members and even non-church members to respond to any sense of vocation to support the work. This could be, for example, joining a visiting team under the guidance of the nurse, participating in the support group for the health ministry, helping with administration or the raising of resources, or providing practical support for a family in need. The interview transcripts show that these kinds of activities are happening in all fifteen parish nurse churches.

One further point needs to made here. Even though it appears that coordination and support for volunteers is not so frequently found in non-parish nurse churches, one cannot assume that the practice of volunteering is less; it may just be more spontaneous and less organized.

## WHOLISTIC MISSION

It has already been argued that for mission to be truly wholistic it needs to include interventions that are to do with physical health, mental health, community health, and spiritual health.

Three of the ministers said they found it difficult to complete the columns for interventions in the way that was requested, but all made some effort to do so. Interestingly, all three of these ministers were from churches with a strongly evangelical tradition.

The survey gave some helpful perspectives on what was happening in mission in the seventy-seven non-parish nurse churches. However, it did not measure the amount of mission activity in any one of the categories. It could be that a particular church was focusing a large amount of missional activity in say, group discussion about faith (e.g. Alpha courses) and consequently not having much church time left to be involved with wider activities.

It has been ascertained in chapter 3 that a key criterion for wholistic or integral mission is that a wide range of missional activities is offered across all four categories. So the research tool measures the range of activities offered, rather than the time given to any one of them.

As with the parish nurse churches, the tool did not identify the relationship of each intervention to one of four categories; it did not therefore encourage ministers to try and engineer a "balanced" response. Instead, the results were grouped subsequently into physical, mental, community, and spiritual health interventions. The percentages of churches engaging in each intervention were then calculated. The following four graphs show the range of interventions in which the seventy-seven churches were involved. They are placed next to the same information from the fifteen churches as recorded in chapter 5. It should be remembered that to represent the percentages of fifteen against the percentages of seventy-seven will be unreliable where differences are minor, but where there are major differential trends these become clear.

## Physical Health Interventions

Figure 17 shows the percentage of control group churches that engaged in twenty-one different physical health interventions alongside the percentage of the fifteen studied parish nurse churches that engaged in the same activities.

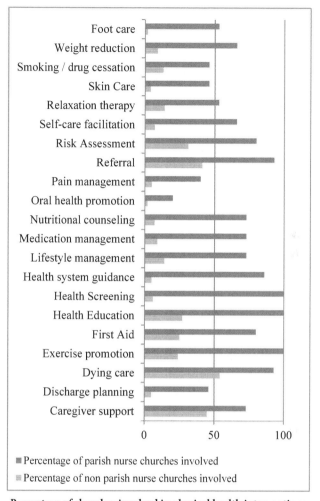

**Percentage of churches involved in physical health interventions**

Although plenty of churches have a theology that inspires social action, few would include physical health interventions as part of that understanding, so, as one might expect, the range of physical health care interventions recorded by ministers without parish nurses are notably less than in the parish nurse churches. The figures are 17 percent of possible interventions in the control group, compared to 70 percent in the parish nurse group. The nurses involved in the fifteen churches were all specialists in physical health, so this major difference in physical health interventions is to be expected.

However, it is clear that a significant proportion of churches without a parish nurse are involved in referral, dying care, and caregiver support. Other physical interventions are less common, probably because most of them require some professional knowledge that may not be available within the church congregation.

## Mental Health Interventions

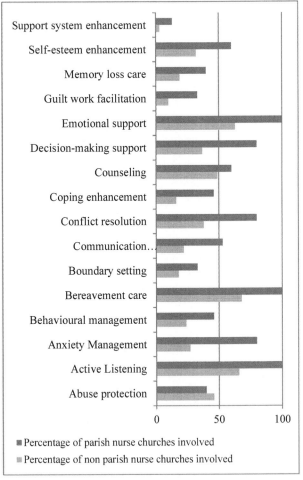

■ Percentage of parish nurse churches involved
■ Percentage of non parish nurse churches involved

**Percentage of churches engaged in mental health interventions**

Figure 18 shows the percentage of control churches that engaged in sixteen mental health interventions. Again this is set alongside the corresponding figure for parish nurse churches. In the control group churches, there is involvement in 34 percent of the total possible interventions compared to 60 percent of total possible interventions in the parish nurse churches.

Here, it is evident that more churches are engaged in mental health work than in physical health. The most common such interventions by non-parish nurse churches are emotional support, counseling, bereavement care, active listening, and abuse protection. Given that professional expertise in these areas may not often be present in the congregations, this is a significant contribution by churches to mental wellbeing. All of the parish nurses in the survey were general nurses, not mental health nurses, although there are other parish nurses who are mental health specialists. What is surprising, therefore, is that with the exception of abuse protection, which is usually led by two named individuals in a church, the parish nurse churches were even more commonly involved in all of these mental health interventions. This included particular attention to emotional support, conflict resolution, decision-making support, bereavement care, anxiety management, and active listening, even if, as figure 6 (in chapter 5) shows, it was not necessarily the parish nurse herself that was involved.

## Community Health Interventions

Engaging with the community has become a key phrase in contemporary church mission and so one might expect there to be a greater involvement in this kind of intervention by the seventy-seven churches. One might also hope that many of the churches would be involved in justice or environmental issues for individuals or groups, and this should feature under advocacy for the individual or the community. The results show that some of the churches are indeed engaged in various community issues, but not as many as expected. The most common interventions in the seventy-seven churches are relationship building and networking.

Yet there is significant increase for fourteen of the community interventions in the fifteen parish nurse churches; all of them have involvement with end of life issues, and 90 percent of them engage with support of volunteers, networking, relationship building, and family support. They are also more often involved with crisis intervention, advocacy, and even employment issues, although in the last case, it is not the parish nurse herself that is intervening. (see figure 7 in chapter 5)

In total, the control group churches report involvement in 32 percent of the possible community health interventions, compared to involvement in 67 percent of the possible community health interventions in the parish nurse churches.

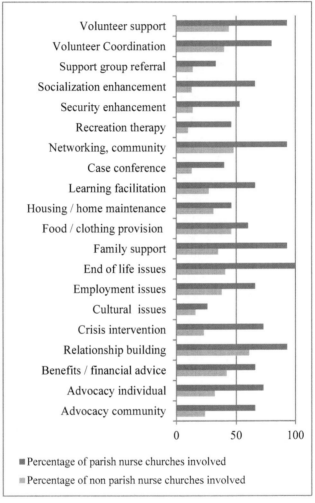

**Percentage of churches engaged in community health interventions**

## Spiritual Health Interventions

This is the area in which one might expect the seventy-seven churches to be extremely active. For some churches, from a variety of traditions, this may be the only area for which they have developed a theological rationale. The results have shown that a majority of the seventy-seven churches are involved in all eleven interventions except for spiritual abuse protection, meditation and forgiveness facilitation. There are two interventions that offered some unexpected results at first glance. It might be thought that every church would be involved in individual discussions about faith or group discussions about faith. According to these results, that was not the case. That may be due to theological stance. Neither the parish nurse churches nor the control churches were differentiated according to their theological position.

A comparison with the parish nurse churches shows that yet again, parish nurse churches are more involved in spiritual care interventions than the non-parish nurse churches. In total, the control group churches were engaged in 55 percent of the possible total spiritual health interventions, compared to involvement in 80 percent of the possible spiritual health interventions in the parish nurse churches.

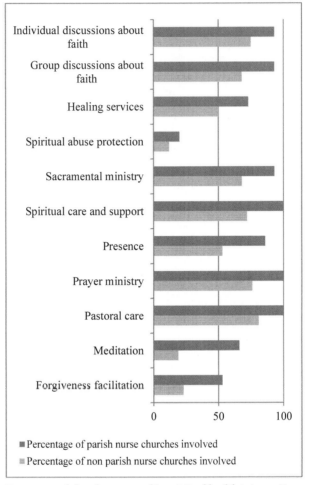

**Percentage of churches engaged in spiritual health interventions**

## Total Interventions

The range of interventions in all four categories of mission is markedly increased in the parish nurse churches. In the control group, there is involvement in 32 percent of the total possible interventions. In the parish nurse churches there is involvement in 68 percent of the total possible interventions. This is seen even more clearly if the number of interventions ticked in each category is plotted against the possible number of interventions for that category. Figure 21 illustrates this.

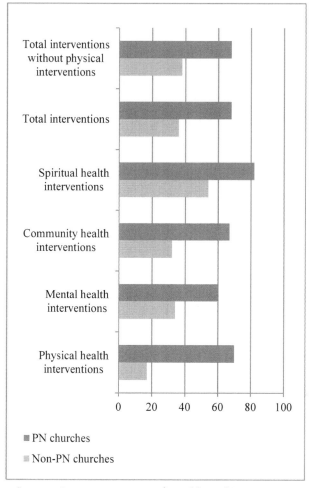

Total interventions
without physical
interventions

Total interventions

Spiritual health
interventions

Community health
interventions

Mental health
interventions

Physical health
interventions

0    20    40    60    80    100

■ PN churches
▩ Non-PN churches

**Interventions as a percentage of possible total interventions**

## EXTENDING GOD'S KINGDOM

All of the above could be argued to be relevant missional activities, even
if the clients concerned were church-goers and even if they were already
believers. Such an argument would focus around the need for church members to be fit, healthy, emotionally stable, living in community with one another and spiritually aware so that they can engage in God's Kingdom work.
That work may not specifically be on behalf of the church but will give them
opportunities to be good witnesses for Christ, in deed and/or word.

But in chapter 3 it was established that the mission task of the church is to share the whole gospel of God, and if that is not possible in its entirety in the "secular" sphere, then there is also a rationale for church-based work that serves people who are not churchgoers. In other words, there is a place for believers to be involved in Kingdom work that extends from the church, into whatever may be defined as its community, *on behalf of* the church. Flett refers to this as the "point of connection," a term used in a previous generation in a foreign missions context, but relevant again today in the relationship between church and secular world.[1] So how much church time is spent in this way? Ministers were asked to estimate within a percentage of possible church time (i.e., the amount of time given to church work by both staff and congregation). As indicated in chapter 4, this question (10) was not an easy question for ministers to answer. Four of the seventy-seven commented that they had found it difficult. They all however filled it in.

1. Flett, *Witness of God*, 166.

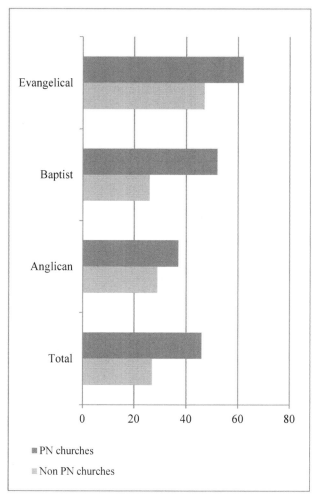

**Average church time spent with non-church people**

The answers they gave were then calculated in average form. That is, where a figure of 10–25 percent was given, the median value, 17.5 percent was noted and the whole column averaged.

The average percentage of time spent working with or for people who are not regular church attendees on behalf of the church was 27 percent in the seventy-seven non-parish nurse churches. That compares with 46 percent in the fifteen churches with parish nurses.

It could be said that Anglican churches might normally spend more time with non-churchgoers because of their ecclesiology, so it was decided to look more closely at these comparisons. A breakdown of the numbers between Anglicans and Baptists did indeed show that Anglicans reported spending more time with non-churchgoers than Baptists. Perhaps the definition of who is or is not a churchgoer is less clear in an Anglican ecclesiology. But in the churches with parish nurses there was a clear increase in time spent with people who did not normally attend church, whatever the denomination. In Baptist churches, the increase in time was greater.

Would geographical context make a difference to the amount of time spent with non-church people? For example, did churches in a rural area spend more time with non-church people in the community than churches in a suburban area? To answer that, comparisons were made between like for like churches.

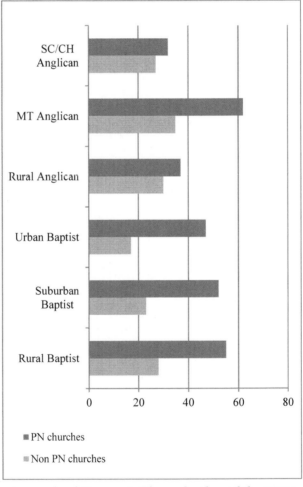

**Average church time spent with non-church people by context**

There was no question in the survey directly relating to the offering of God's salvation, but there were two questions about discussion of faith issues: 68 percent of the non-parish nurse churches were involved in group discussion about faith, compared to 100 percent of the fifteen parish nurse churches; and 75 percent of the non-parish nurse churches were involved in individual discussion about faith, compared to 100 percent of the fifteen parish nurse churches.

## OFFERING CHOICE

In chapter 3 it was argued that those involved in Christian mission activity do not have any biblical authority to exert pressure on vulnerable people. There was no specific question on this in the survey of seventy-seven churches. Experience from working with one hundred and fifty churches in mission suggests that most do offer people choice. In the past, people may have been invited to church activities that were advertised as purely social events, and then be subject to preaching as part of the same event. This is no longer common practice.

Church health activities are not directly connected to state information systems. This brings with it the privilege of serving people who might not otherwise access state health and social care for fear of authority: asylum seekers, for example, homeless people, and migrant workers. These are vulnerable members of society and churches need to be very careful not to exert pressure to convert or "join up" on them. They need to demonstrate this by making referrals to other bodies where appropriate, given the permission of the client. In the survey, 40 percent of the comparative churches and 90 percent of the parish nurse churches were making such referrals. The skill of referring patients appropriately is one with which that nurses are familiar, and so this result is not surprising. It does however indicate that the parish nurses in the study are likely to be practicing with the principle of offering choice.

In addition, all the parish nurses involved in the study, and those practicing anywhere else, are encouraged to develop leaflets that explain where they are from, who they are working for, and what they can offer. Each client receives this and has the choice to accept or decline the care. That choice is not always available when working from the state-funded NHS; hence the public concern about nurses working for the NHS who might use the opportunity to "evangelize."

## INTEGRATION OF EVANGELISM
## AND SOCIAL ENGAGEMENT

Again, there was no question on this in the survey of comparative churches. But anecdotal evidence from the churches where the researcher and some of her colleagues have conducted mission consultancies suggests a division between the kind of activities that meet social need, for example toddler groups, and lunch clubs, and the kind of activities that teach about faith.[2] Indeed, the discussion about offering choice, above, might lead a church to believe that the two activities should be kept separate. This is a not uncommon view. It is supported in part, for stage one "preparing" activities by the popular *Sowing, Reaping, Keeping* strategy for evangelism, developed by Lawrence Singlehurst.[3] It should be noted though, that Singlehurst advises this in the context of encouraging churches to offer a program of separate but intentionally related events that may be taken by the visitors at their own discretion. When attended in succession, the spiritual content of the subsequent events might enable a person to find faith for themselves.

The offer of wholistic health care led by a parish nurse working from a local church means that people receive professional advice on physical, mental or community health care, and where appropriate, this is given along with the offer of some discussion of faith issues or prayer. If the client wishes, this may happen in the same visit. But there is no pressure to do this if the client declines. As already noted, the statistics submitted by parish nurses for 2010 show that in 52 percent of consultations, prayer was not offered.

In the parish nurse introductory course, parish nurses learn how to assess clients from a wholistic perspective, using models that include biblical values, like justice, forgiveness and serving others. The resultant care plan is therefore a truly integrated one. As the 2010 Lausanne commitment suggests, this is both proclamation and demonstration of the gospel, in an example of integrated mission.[4]

---

2. In England, this division is not enforced by government, but is demanded by some funders.

3. Singlehurst, *Sowing, Reaping, Keeping*.

4. Lausanne, "Cape Town Commitment," 11–12.

## COMPARISON OF FINDINGS IF THE SMALL CHURCHES ARE REMOVED FROM THE CONTROL GROUP

In chapter 4, it was noted that the self-selected control group of seventy-six churches included twenty churches with a regular congregational attendance of less than fifty.[5] Since none of the parish nurse churches had congregations as low as that, this factor may be of significant influence in the results from the control group. A second look was therefore taken at the comparisons with the control group excluding those twenty small churches.

The number of churches that had health professionals in their congregation in the seventy-seven control group churches was fifty-nine. (76 percent) If the twenty smaller churches were removed from the group the figure is forty-nine of the remaining fifty-seven churches. So the percentage goes up to 85 percent of congregations that include at least one health professional.

The control group responses from the survey tool to question B62 about involvement in volunteer coordination give a figure of 40 percent. If the small churches are taken out, this figure changes to 45 percent, so an increase is noted. However when this is compared to the 80 percent of parish nurses churches engaged in volunteer coordination, there is still a very significant difference.

Volunteer support, question B63, showed 44 percent involvement in the control group churches. When small churches are removed from the sample, the figure changes to 47 percent. Again, this is a slight increase, perhaps explained by the fact that smaller churches have fewer volunteers that might need support. But as 93 percent of parish nurse churches are engaged in this activity, there is still an obvious variance.

The total number of categories ticked by the control group churches gives a figure of just over 31 percent of possible interventions. If the small churches are taken out, the equivalent figure is 33 percent, so there is little difference there in comparison to the 68 percent of total interventions recorded by the ministers of the parish nurse churches.

But is there a difference in the type of interventions if small churches are removed from the control group? For physical health interventions, the difference is 2 percent more (19 percent), for mental health interventions 1 percent more (35 percent), for community health interventions 2 percent more (34 percent), and for spiritual health interventions 2 percent more (57

5. See chapter 4.

percent). So in comparison to the parish nurse church figures of 70 percent, 60 percent, 67 percent, and 80 percent, the differences are not significant.

When it comes to referrals, there is more of a difference in the control group if the small churches are taken out of the calculations: the figure of 40 percent responses to category B48 in the seventy-seven churches becomes 49 percent of the fifty-seven churches. But again, this is dwarfed by the responses to that category in the parish nurse churches: 93 percent of them make referrals to other agencies.

There is an interesting but small variation when comparing the average amount of time spent with people outside the church on behalf of the church. When the small churches are taken out, this actually reduces. Instead of 27 percent of church time being spent with people outside the church in the seventy-seven churches, it is actually lower if the small churches are taken out: 26 percent of the fifty-seven churches. Does this mean that small churches spend more time with people outside of the church? This concept of church time spent with those who do not attend demands further attention. Perhaps this is a subject for further study. However, for the purposes of this work, the average time spent on behalf of the church with those who are not regular attendees is much higher in the parish nurse churches: 46 percent.

Removing the smaller churches from the control group produces minor differences in the results. It does not, however, diminish the contrast between control group and parish nurse churches by any meaningful amount.

# 7

# Significance of the Findings

Given the opportunity for care of the whole person that parish nursing offers, one might expect it to have some impact on the church's outreach. What conclusions can be reached on the basis of this research?

## ESTABLISHED RESULTS

All fifteen ministers of the fifteen churches with parish nurses were in agreement that the appointment of a parish nurse had helped them to increase their mission activities. Eight of these were strongly in agreement. All fifteen were also keen to recommend that other churches appoint parish nurses, in order to enhance their mission involvement. Twelve of these registered strong agreement with this statement. The ministers obviously believe that it does make a difference. That is a very strong recommendation, because many of them will have invested time and money into other missional activities with which they will have compared parish nursing. In addition to the confidence shown by these ministers who have personally worked with the nurses, the evidence has clearly shown that the appointment of a parish nurse has an effect on three specific aspects of a church's mission.

## Time Spent with People Who Do Not Attend Church

It has been seen that the average of church time spent working with or for people who are not regular church attendees on behalf of the church was 27 percent in the control group of seventy-seven non parish nurse churches, but 46 percent in the parish nurse churches. It should be noted that this was total time spent by any or all of the church members and staff, not just the parish nurse. However, this does seem to be a major difference in those churches that have a parish nurse. The evidence suggests that the appointment of a parish nurse almost doubles the amount of time spent with non-church people.

Could this be explained by the possibility that those churches were more involved in outreach even before they had a nurse? Might it be that their interest in community engagement was one of the reasons for them making the appointment in the first place? Perhaps so, but in the statistical information from thirty-four parish nurses in thirty-one churches for 2010, it is clear that parish nurses do spend at least 25 percent of their personal consultation time with people who do not attend church regularly. That does not include the time spent doing health education, training volunteers, or participating in healing services that may be specially timed and planned for people who do not normally attend church. Neither does it include the time spent engaging with people who work for other voluntary agencies, or with those who work for the health services, many of whom may not be churchgoers. So it could be expected that the appointment of a parish nurse would increase the amount of church time spent with non-church people.

It was also interesting to note that all fifteen ministers agreed that the church's liaison with other voluntary organizations had increased, seven of them strongly so. This would add further weight to the finding that a church's engagement with people outside of its congregation was increased in the parish nurse churches. Liaison with other voluntary organizations might also be increased by the appointment of other workers, for example family workers, whose specific job description asked that they work with outside agencies, but that does not alter the fact that these results show that a parish nurse appointment does bring the church more into contact with those who are not part of it.

In chapter 3, one of the key features of the mission of a local church was the extension of God's reign, and the offer of his salvation amongst people that do not yet know him.[1] It can at least be said that the appointment of a parish nurse increased the amount of church-based contact with people who did not attend church regularly. Some of these people may have been followers of Christ, or at least God-fearers who just had not yet found ways of connecting or re-connecting with a local church. But there is a strong possibility that some may not have known him. And among these people, with their permission, the parish nurse has brought the church's message of God's love for them, his care for their bodies and his offer of hope for their futures. In many of the examples, the parish nurse had the privilege of praying for them. In most cases, however, this had been at best an introductory stage in faith development. It had not led to a full explanation of the gospel, the opportunity for repentance and baptism, or the invitation to become a regular church member. These are later stages in a journey to faith that may be facilitated by other sections of the church. The notable exception is found in the interview transcript from PN14, the nurse who gave her interview towards the end of the study period. In a future study it would be interesting to find out whether or not other clients in other churches had subsequently taken further steps of faith.

The number of opportunities for people outside of the church to have contact with it is reducing in the UK, due to the closure or amalgamation of many small and/or rural churches, over the last twenty years, the reduction of the number of weekly services offered at convenient times, and reduced clergy availability. This initial outreach by the church, this potential for connection with the local church, is of deep significance in a context where most people do not normally have that contact.

## Volunteering

The second aspect of a church's mission that was clearly different in the parish nurse churches was the increase in the coordination and support of volunteers. These people helped in all kinds of ways, from serving tea and coffee to those waiting in the parish nurse clinic, to finding funding for the ongoing activities, providing transport for hospital visits, or helping to organize a health fair. When a parish nurse came across a family that needed temporary or long-term practical help she/he relied on volunteers to supply that help. Some nurses worked with teams of pastoral care volunteers that regularly visited older people and referred back to the parish nurse if

---

1. See Chapter 3.

medical knowledge was needed. Some of those volunteers may even have been other clients, service-users not linked in other ways with the church, but who found that volunteering helped them to feel a sense of purpose and dignity. This fulfils the vision outlined in the Cape Town meeting of the Lausanne movement referred to in chapter 3.

Churches depend on volunteers of all kinds. Most have pastoral care teams, even if only for their own members. As previously seen, it cannot be assumed from these results that parish nurse churches have numerically more volunteers, although the evidence does seem to point in that direction. The presence of a parish nurse clearly makes a difference to the coordination and support of volunteers. In the parish nurse churches, 80 percent of the ministers said they or a congregation member, (which may or may not have been the parish nurse), spent time spent coordinating volunteers. And 93 percent said they or a congregation member spent time supporting volunteers. In the control group, the corresponding figures were 40 and 44 percent, or 45 and 47 percent without the smaller churches. This is a major difference. It may not be because the control group churches had fewer volunteers; however, it may indicate that there was a less organized approach to the coordination and support of those volunteers.

There is a limited amount of time that any congregation member can give in volunteering. Even those who are retired usually have family responsibilities to cover. It may be that what was happening in the parish nurse churches was not recruitment of fresh volunteers, but rather that people were drawn away from whatever they might otherwise have volunteered to do and move towards the parish nurse ministry. This could be a cause of concern for other parts of the church's work, unless of course, the health ministry is seen as a more effective use of time from a missional perspective.

Another of the theological aspects of mission from a local church discussed in chapter three was the release and deployment of every member as they experience a sense of God's call to ministries of various kinds. It would seem that parish nursing encourages this not only in offering nurses the opportunity to further explore their vocation, but in facilitating the further engagement of volunteers. The parish nurse churches had a more organized approach to this, which may help to explain why the average number of volunteers per nurse per year in the 2010 statistics was as high as seventeen.

Such an increase in volunteer work is probably not unique to parish nursing. It could happen with other staff workers appointed with a job description that includes the recruitment and coordination of volunteers, for example, with a youth worker who runs a holiday club. But it clearly also happens with the appointment of a parish nurse.

## Range of Activities

Another aspect of a church's mission where significant difference has been shown in these results relates to the range of activities with which church or congregation members are engaged, on behalf of the church. The tool that was developed in order to explore this range of interventions was completed by the ministers in both groups and was the same for the parish nurse churches as for the control group.

All of the parish nurses in this study were registered general nurses rather than registered mental health nurses. But contrary to any expectation that the presence of a general trained parish nurse would only increase the amount or range of physical health activities, the research shows that in the parish nurse churches, there was a marked increase in the range of all possible interventions—spiritual, mental and community, as well as physical. Furthermore, the increase was not significantly affected by removing the smaller churches from the control sample.

If, as was discussed in chapter 3, a third feature of the mission of a local church is that it is involved in activities that promote physical, mental, social, and spiritual health, then these results seem to indicate that the appointment of a parish nurse could significantly increase the range of interventions across all four categories. This means that someone coming into contact with a local church through one activity is able to access other types of intervention that relate to whole person care. Such praxis reflects the theological understanding of *shalom* in the Old Testament and the *zoe* of the New Testament referred to in chapter 3.

## IMPLIED RESULTS

A number of additional factors have been mentioned in the ministers and parish nurse interviews that would seem to relate to the remaining two missional criteria. These cannot be compared with the control group because the same interviews could not be conducted with churches without parish nurses.

The fourth criterion was the offer of choice. The researcher would need to be present in a nurse/client intervention to know whether or not choice was being offered, or to conduct separate interviews with the client, so any kind of result concerning respect for freewill would be difficult to confirm without such evidence. However, the impression conveyed by most of the ministers and most of the nurses did seem to indicate that they felt that the free will of the clients was being respected. This perspective is supported by the fact that a health and exercise club was organized by a parish nurse for the benefit of Muslim women on church premises, without any intent to convert (M2), and that health education was offered unconditionally to a group that had no church connections (M6). In both these cases it seemed that the experience of the nurse in respecting choice about faith issues within the NHS helped the church to have confidence in adopting such an approach.

The fifth criterion, another of the key features of a local church's mission discussed in chapter three, was the concept of integral mission. The work of a parish nurse would seem to embody this principle. It was noted in chapter 2 that integration of faith and prayer is a key aspect of a parish nurse's work, being one of the internationally agreed seven common functions. The integration of social action with discussion about faith and prayer was apparent in thirteen of the fifteen parish nurse interviews and referred to in eleven of the ministers' transcripts. Since the control group was not interviewed, no similar question was asked, so it was not possible to make comparisons.

Although it is strictly against a nurse's professional code of practice to put pressure on any client with regard to discussing matters of faith, spiritual care needs to form part of the nurse's assessment of the client's health condition, and this may lead to questions of a spiritual nature. Reference to faith or prayer was recorded in almost half of all personal consultations in the 2010 statistics from thirty-four nurses. This would imply that whilst the integration of faith-word and faith-action does not happen in every interpersonal conversation, it is both normal and common in the practice of a parish nurse. This is significant because in the experience of the researcher such integration is not necessarily normal and common in every church-based social outreach activity.

## SIGNIFICANCE FOR CHURCHES
## WITHOUT PARISH NURSES

Important implications have arisen from this work for churches that do not yet have parish nurses. These relate to the extension of God's Kingdom, the release and deployment of members, and engagement in truly wholistic mission.

## The Extension of God's Reign

In chapter 3 it was established that the church is invited to share in God's mission task of extending his Kingdom. A quotation from Karl Barth was cited to emphasize that in the act of receiving God the (sending) Spirit, the church has not only the command of Jesus to go and make disciples of all nations, but is enabled to do this through the characteristic of the indwelling power of God.

Flett highlights some of the differences between the theological position of Barth and the missiological contribution of Brunner.[2] He sees a weakness in Barth's dogmatics, namely a repudiation of natural theology, a split between God's being and God's particular act, so that there is tendency for the church to focus in on herself and her relationship with Christ, rather than God and his relationship with the world. Barth himself refers to what is seen by Flett as an outcome of the breach between what is divine and what is human.

> It is painful to have to admit, and it is a serious indictment of our established European churches, that in the main this (devotion to mission) is to be found only in external organizations and the so-called sects, and that in the great churches it is usually encountered only among those who belong to special societies, and not in the congregations as such, in which it seems to be tacitly suspected as fanatical, intolerant, and interfering.[3]

This is significant for English churches because Barth's admission can be clearly demonstrated in the later twentieth century; during this period it became the common tendency of the church to divert her missionary-minded congregational members toward a suitable missionary agency along with some financial resources and thus divest herself of her own

2. Flett, *Witness of God*, 166.
3. Ibid., 165.

responsibilities for wholistic mission within her locality. For example, why has it often been the case that any nurse discerning a call to combine physical care with spiritual care has been sent off to another part of the world to work for a missionary agency rather than use his or her skills with the local church? And why, on their return, have they often been required to develop other skills, such as Sunday school teaching, in order to become useful in the local church?

Flett attempts to reconstruct the concept of *Missio Dei,* bringing together the insights of Brunner and Barth to offer a Trinitarian context for mission, the human/divine breach being overcome through God, Father, Son, and Spirit, three in one, reconciling the world to Himself.[4] He concludes, "The Christian community is a missionary community, for, if she is not, then she is not the community of God's reconciliation."[5]

In the seventy-seven churches that formed the control group in this study, the average amount of church time spent with people who did not attend church was only 27 percent. For the Baptist churches, the amount of time spent in this way was slightly lower than in the Anglican churches. Five churches from a variety of denominations, contexts and sizes, registered less than 10 percent of time spent in this way, and thirty churches of all kinds registered less than 25 percent of church time spent with non-church people. It could be argued that if members of those churches are both acting and speaking the gospel in their everyday working lives, without seeing that as part of church time, then the church is clearly engaging with God's mission in the world, albeit in a somewhat distanced way. But if the world in which they are engaged does not permit discussion about faith, and people do not attend church of their own volition, then the question of how people are to hear the gospel remains a major issue.

Flett also quotes Brunner, who was writing at around the same time as Barth, but from missionary experience rather than dogmatic theology. He foresaw the secularization of Europe as the collapse of Christendom began, and urged that action be taken,

> Drawing on the tremendous treasure of experience and insight acquired from two hundred years of practice . . . in preaching the gospel to the heathen, teaching their children, engaging in their individual pastoral care, forming communities among them, and penetrating the peoples with the spirit of the gospel . . . (The

4. Ibid., 196–239.
5. Ibid., 290.

missionary weighed) which mechanisms of the practical life, which orders of the social life, prove themselves to be valuable starting points and bases, and which prove to be the opposite.[6]

But if so little church time is being spent with people who do not attend services, and if people do not attend of their own accord, then how are these "mechanisms of the practical life" to be identified and evaluated? One such mechanism is in the area of health. The appointment of a parish nurse would appear to be one way of discovering whether or not health care in the community is a valuable starting point. However, it must not be assumed that this automatically will lead to conversions, because the nurse does not engage in what is normally termed "evangelism." Indeed, when asked whether people had come to faith as a result of parish nurse interventions, almost half of the ministers disagreed. It would be interesting to see whether this answer would be different when the nurses had been in post for a longer period of time.

The "Engel scale" has been used in evangelical work in recent years to help churches identify the stage of belief at which an individual may be, so that appropriate action may be taken to help that individual move towards repentance and faith in Christ for themselves.[7] It is a rather inaccurate measure, because people do not necessarily follow the same route to faith, but the scale begins at minus ten for those who have no concept at all of spiritual existence, and moves towards the pivotal point of zero at the moment of confession of Jesus Christ as Lord. It then increases stage by stage through baptism, discipleship, witness, and towards maturity in Christ. It may be helpful here because it enables us to see where the ministry of parish nursing fits where faith development is concerned; given that the service seeks to meet the needs of those who may already have some nominal belief in God and a little knowledge of the gospel, but have not as yet understood any implications of it for their own life, it is most likely to of help to those at minus four and five on the Engel scale. If a church were to develop a parish nurse ministry, there would need to be other activities that address the needs of people who are beyond minus six, for example Alpha courses or the like, that would help those who so desired to explore faith further.

6. Ibid., 167.

7. "Engel Scale," *Christian Medical Fellowship.* The Engel Scale was first published in 1975, in Engel and Wilbert-Norton, *What's gone wrong with the harvest?* It has since been used and quoted in many titles. It is helpfully explained on the website of the Christian Medical Fellowship.

## The Release and Deployment of Members

A further area that may be of significance for churches without parish nurses is the extent to which they manage and support their volunteers. Since most churches cannot exist without volunteers, the assumption has to be made that in the majority (60 percent) of the non-parish nurse churches these people offered their time freely but their work was not formally managed and they were not supported in it. Would the mission of the church be more effectively accomplished if these volunteers were coordinated and/ or supported appropriately? Or is there perhaps a fear that they would withdraw their service if they felt they had to do their work in a more accountable way? The evidence from the parish nurse churches, where 80 per cent and 93 per cent of the ministers recorded that time was spent in coordinating and supporting volunteers, is that this does not result in loss of people's willingness to help. Rather, the evidence from the interviews in the parish nurse churches suggests that in the majority of them, volunteering increased.

## Wholistic Mission

In chapter 3 the case was made that mission needs to be wholistic, and that interventions might need to be made across the spectrum from physical to mental to community to spiritual activities. The tool developed to test this did not divide the categories of intervention; they were randomly distributed in the questionnaire, and only separated out by the researcher subsequent to the completion of the questionnaires, but before the results were entered.

Only 17 percent of the ministers in the control group marked physical interventions as part of their church's activities. The areas in which they were most commonly involved were dying care, caregiver support, risk assessment, and referral. These results were to be expected, given that in the last sixty years an English church has not normally been associated with involvement in such things as skin care, nutritional counseling, or health screening. These things have been taken care of through the National Health Service. Yet if they are a "mechanism of the practical life" to quote Brunner again, is there perhaps some advantage in re-engaging with some of these activities, to the extent that the church is able to participate in them? The results clearly show that the appointment of a parish nurse will assist with this, but that is not to discount other ways in which physical interventions can be offered.

Churches in the control group, without parish nurses, were more significantly involved in mental health activities than physical health activities. The findings in this survey would be of great interest to those responsible for mental health care in England, because they demonstrate that a church can be an important source of support for people who could be at risk of mental illness. This is particularly seen in bereavement care and emotional support, where 60 percent of the churches were involved. Again, however, the results have shown that the appointment of a parish nurse suggested an increase in nearly all the mental health interventions. All of the parish nurse churches were engaged in emotional support, bereavement care, and active listening.

The percentage of churches in the control group engaged in community health interventions varied from 10 percent in recreation therapy to 60 percent in relationship building. Over 40 percent recorded involvement in food and clothing provision, benefits or financial advice, and community networking. But again, those with a parish nurse as part of their team recorded involvement in a higher percentage of community health activities, notably at both the beginning (family support) and end of life.

One would expect that most churches would be involved in spiritual health, and this was indeed where the control group scored most highly. Pastoral care, prayer ministry, spiritual care and support, sacramental ministry, group discussions about faith, and individual discussions about faith, all featured strongly. But even here, in every case, a higher percentage of the churches with parish nurses recorded involvement in each spiritual health intervention.

There are many varieties of ministries that will increase a church's activities in particular interventions. A family worker for example may increase a church's involvement in family support, food and clothing provision, or benefits and financial advice. A youth worker may increase the church's involvement in many of these interventions with young people. A person appointed to visit the elderly may greatly affect the church's engagement with bereavement care or socialization enhancement. Further work would need to be done to see if the appointment of such people had a similar overall effect as that of a parish nurse: increasing the percentage of interventions across the whole range of possible activities.

## SIGNIFICANCE FOR CHURCHES WITH PARISH NURSES

It has been demonstrated that the appointment of a parish nurse may help a church to increase its involvement in the five missional criteria that were identified in chapter 3 of this work: the release and deployment of members, involvement in a broader range of interventions, engagement with people who do not attend church, the offer of choice, and integral mission. However, as indicated in the discussion around the "Engel scale" above, the pre-interview surveys revealed that nearly half of the ministers disagreed with the statement that people had come to faith, partly as a result of parish nurse interventions. This highlights the fact that parish nursing is not of itself an evangelistic activity. It may lead to a person wanting to find out more about faith, but there will need to be other means by which they may do that. Churches with parish nurses will need to ensure that these means are available, or they may find that the opportunities for faith development offered to people through parish nursing will not be taken up.

Some of the interviews also revealed the offer of advocacy, and so issues of justice have sometimes been addressed. Conflict resolution featured in 80 percent of the parish nurse churches, and forgiveness facilitation featured in over 50 percent of them, so the divine value of peacemaking was often present. However, very little mention was made of the concern for God's creation, which was one of the divine values that should be evident in the missional work of the church. Perhaps parish nurses and/or their volunteers need to begin to address environmental issues as they relate to the work they do. For example, does the parish nurse use a bicycle rather than a car, do the church's facilities take account of the need to use energy sparingly, and does the church help the community make the most of recycling opportunities?

Another "divine value" that was not referred to in the interviews was that of prophetic engagement with political issues, such as the environmental causes of ill-health, or the commercially-driven aspects of research in the causes of disease. Advocacy on behalf of the community was one of the intervention categories however and featured in 65 percent of the parish nurse churches, compared to 23 percent of the non-parish nurse churches, so perhaps the parish nurses are engaged in political activity to some extent.

The fifteen churches studied had all been working with a parish nurse for at least eighteen months, and some of the interview transcripts indicated a development during that time as the nurse gained confidence, extended networks, and recruited volunteers. This seems to point to the need for a nurse to take time to grow the ministry, and so confirms the policy with which parish nursing in the UK was commenced: that in negotiating an appointment, a period of at least three years is desirable. This was anticipated from the beginning and in every application the church signs an agreement that it intends to run the project for at least three years.

The interview transcripts indicated a positive response to the outcomes on the part of both the ministers and the parish nurses, even though not many had recorded instances of conversions or new church members. Such a view would appear to be supported by Tom Wright, who, in writing about hope, sees all work done towards the building of God's kingdom as valuable investment in what is to come.[8] He likens this to the work of a master architect who enlists craftsmen to work at features that will one day be used to form part of the large building he is working on. In describing Wright's theology, Stephen Kuhrt notes that it implies a lasting impact to "every piece of kingdom work built on the foundation of Jesus." He tells how Wright's perspective has engendered a more wholistic approach to mission in his own church, inspiring those who see themselves as "do-ers and carers" rather than theologians.[9] According to this view, parish nursing would seem therefore to be an intrinsically valuable activity, even if it never produced more conversions or church members.

A concern that was raised more than once in the interviews was that of succession planning. How would this work be continued once the nurses concerned had retired? In one of the churches the nurse had already moved away and despite a deep desire for a replacement, no new appointment had been made. However, some of the work she had initiated was continuing. This is a deeply significant factor for the churches with parish nurses. If the work is seen as valuable to the community it is important that potential new recruits are sought and mentored so that it can be sustained. Funding may need to be accessed in order to offer paid hours to any future parish nurse. In addition to local efforts, there is plainly a need for the charity PNMUK to be more pro-active in seeking to recruit new nurses to parish nursing. If no nurses are available, then the volunteers need to be trained to continue the work at least to the level of their competence. It may be that arrangements can be made for their supervision from a nearby parish nurse church.

8. Wright, *Surprised by Hope*, 220–21.
9. Kuhrt, *Tom Wright*, 75–76.

## SIGNIFICANCE FOR NURSES

In chapter 1 it was claimed that the ministry of parish nursing could address three areas of influence. The third of these was the main focus of this study and it has been seen that the appointment of a parish nurse may encourage churches to restore the health and healing mission of the gospel in a variety of ways. But the first area of influence was that it could help nurses to reclaim the spiritual dimension of health care. A glance at the application forms of those who want to train as parish nurses reveals that this is something very important to them. Throughout the fifteen interviews it became clear that not only did the nurses see their own calling as a vocation from God, but that through this ministry they were able to do something that they were not given time to do within the NHS; to attend to a person's spiritual needs as well as their physical, mental or community needs. Many of them saw this as fulfilling their original vocation: to try to bring a sense of wholeness, healing and wellbeing to people throughout their life circumstances. All of the nurses in the study except for PN2 were working within churches with which they were previously involved in other ways. PN2 had been very loosely involved with a larger congregation, having had other family and work responsibilities that prevented her from regular commitments. Might it be possible in the future that churches looking for parish nurses draw in those Christian nurses who for various reasons have stopped coming regularly to church? And by that means, perhaps help them to restore their sense of calling?

## SIGNIFICANCE FOR THE UK HEALTH SERVICES

The second area of influence was the encouragement of health care systems to treat the patient as a whole. The NHS has recently undergone yet another re-organization. It is hoped that this will enhance its ability to be more wholistic in its approach to patient care, but staffing and resources may limit this. It is noteworthy that since parish nursing has begun in the UK, there has been greater interest in spiritual care within the nursing world: two major nursing conferences on the subject have been held by the *Nursing Standard*, and speakers from parish nursing have featured in both of these. Some General Practitioners have begun to introduce chaplains to their surgeries. This interest is partly due to the work of eminent academics that have recognized the need for greater attention to spiritual care, but also perhaps to the contribution of complementary medicine in highlighting alternative spiritualities. It may be a reaction to the secularization of the state-funded NHS that discourages a nurse from engaging in conversation about matters of faith in his or her NHS workplace.

In chapter 1 it was recognized that this focus on spiritual care is not without controversy. Some contributors would prefer to use the term psycho-social care. They warn against the use of the term spiritual care in the NHS, in case religious groups might see it as authority to promote their faith amongst vulnerable non-believers. Parish nurses work from churches, not from the NHS. Their focus is not the offer of Christian spiritual care to those who would rather not receive it. They make it very clear to clients that they can choose whether or not to receive care from a parish nurse, and whether or not to be referred to a faith group of their choice. So while it is hoped that the NHS will increasingly find ways to treat the patient as a whole, it is not the aim of parish nursing to impose Christian spiritual care on anyone.

A recent meeting with a Public Health officer in the South of England revealed that his health trust had no employees that were specifically targeting the promotion of health among adults, and his view was that any attempt by the churches to help people of middle age live healthier lives would be greatly welcomed. Fifty-nine of the seventy-seven churches without a parish nurse had health professionals as regular attendees at their church. This means that health ministry could be developed at least to some extent through many churches, even if they do not have a registered nurse willing to lead the initiative. Parish Nursing Ministries UK has recently included Occupational Therapists in its training program and other registered health professionals may take the training and join the initiative. They would need to be currently registered with their professional body and whilst they cannot take the title of "Nurse," they can be called, for example, "Parish Physiotherapist." That would increase the number of people who could take up health ministry from churches. However, in the survey it was seen that most of the ministers in the control group did not provide specific support for any of their health professionals. If the health service is to be encouraged to provide more wholistic care, then it will important for these professionals to feel supported by their congregations as they work towards this in a very secular and challenging environment.

In his book, *The Home We Build Together*, Rabbi Jonathan Sacks argues that in order to recreate a sense of society in a divided multicultural context, governments need to protect the social space around covenantal institutions like universities, professional associations, NGO's, charities and churches, where social capital is produced.[10] That means, he says, "empowering charities, voluntary and faith-based groups, some of which may need government funding."[11] He recognizes that this may pose a problem for those governments that are reluctant to offer funding to faith groups but offers the following three principles:

1. Individuals should be free to enter or leave the institution;
2. There is equal provision elsewhere;
3. Such institutions should be based on values compatible with political liberalism.[12]

## SIGNIFICANCE FOR THE MINISTRY OF THE RESEARCHER

In founding and leading the charity Parish Nursing Ministries UK it has been my aim to respond to the contextual mission needs of churches and the training and support needs of nurses in such a way as to establish a sustainable mission-focused ministry. My vision is that the work of the charity will eventually enable at least one church in every large village and town in the UK to offer access to a parish nurse alongside and as a complement to health care provision.

The significant findings that relate to this aim from this research are;

1. The appointment of a parish nurse does seem to enhance the mission of a local church at least in the first eighteen months. Further research needs to be done in order to assess the long-term outcomes in the original fifteen parish nurse churches.

2. This work has only evaluated parish nursing from the perspective of ministers and parish nurses. A different methodology should be developed so that those who have been recipients of parish nursing services can make a contribution to the evaluation.

3. If the missional influence of the appointment of a parish nurse can be as significant as the research as shown, then not only does a

10. Sacks, *Home We Build,* 235.
11. Ibid., 237.
12. Ibid., 237.

sustainable plan for the training and succession of parish nurses in churches need to be maintained, but funding needs to be found for the growth of Parish Nursing Ministries UK. Efforts to attract investment in this next stage of its development have not been very successful in the context of a financial recession and much competition from many other worthy causes. It is hoped that the publication of this work will encourage those with a passing interest to become partners in the initiative.

4. Although the research revealed that some significant contributions were being made in all five of the missional criteria identified in chapter three, mention was also made in that chapter of the need to further the divine values of justice, peace, and respect for God's creation. Justice and forgiveness were occasionally noted but none of the ministers or nurses referred to environmental concerns or prophetic engagement with political concerns. In the future these subjects should be included in the training program, both internationally and in the UK.

5. The conclusions of this research indicate that the mission of the church is indeed furthered through the appointment of a parish nurse. That the being the case, then the profile of the ministry needs to be raised in denominational and nursing publications so that churches and nurses can consider it as a possible option alongside other forms of contemporary mission.

## SIGNIFICANCE FOR MISSION-ENABLERS AND MISSION CONSULTANTS

The fertile ground in which this ministry of parish nursing has been nurtured was the work of mission enabling with one hundred and fifty churches in four counties. One of the features of mission enabling work is the offer of a mission consultancy with a local church, in which the congregation is helped to look at the community needs around its location, and its resources for mission within that catchment area. Various tools have been used to achieve this, including a community surveys, S.W.O.T. charts (strengths, weaknesses, opportunities, and threats) Bible Society church health exercises, and evangelism strategy tools. A more intensive study of the range of missional interventions made by a church has been discovered with the use of the tool that I have developed as part of this research. It offers a view of the breadth of those activities that are undertaken on behalf of the church. In this work, it revealed a few churches to be focusing only on spiritual health activities, and some churches to be lacking in those areas. It also gave churches a glimpse of some of the things they could be doing, that they had not considered before. To this end, the tool would be a useful addition to the resources used for mission consultancy. It does, however, omit any mention of creation care activities, and it would be important to add those to the list of interventions.

# 8

# Rediscovering a Ministry of Health

PARISH NURSING MINISTRY COMMENCED in the UK in November 2003. It involves the appointment of a registered nurse as part of the church ministry team, to work on behalf of the church, developing a whole-person health program with both congregation and community. It has been noted that it claims to contribute to three areas of influence: the field of nursing, the plethora of health care systems, and the role of churches in health. It was the last of these that has been the main attention of this book. For if the initiative is to grow and develop then it is the churches and their leaders that must be convinced of its theological rationale and practical worth in their mission work.

## CONCLUDING REMARKS

The extent to which the initiative of parish nursing has so far been an effective tool in the mission of English churches has been discussed. The objectives of parish nursing as it has been developed in the United States and other countries, have been described; the research surrounding the practice has been reviewed; and the way in which these principles have been applied within the UK context has been outlined. The uniqueness of the role has been explored. Theological literature pertaining to the mission of a local church has been reviewed, and the emerging concept of integral mission as the theme of the latest conference of the Lausanne movement in

Cape Town 2010 has been highlighted. From a survey of missiological writing, five criteria have been derived, along with three divine values, which together have been offered as an evaluative framework for a church's missional activity.

A qualitative study of fifteen churches that have had parish nurses for at least eighteen months has been described. It included a written questionnaire with a broad collection of sixty-eight different interventions with which a church might have been involved as part of its mission activities. Pre-interview surveys were collated and studied, along with the transcripts of semi-structured interviews that were conducted with the ministers of those churches, and (separately) their parish nurses. Information from the 2010 annual statistics collated by Parish Nursing Ministries UK was used to supplement the evidence collected from the pre-interview surveys and the transcripts. The evaluative framework derived from the missiological literature was used to synthesize the results. The findings were compared against completed surveys using the same framework for a questionnaire with a random control group of seventy-seven churches. As a by-product of the research, the framework has also proved to be a useful tool for measuring the breadth and nature of a church's activities in mission and may be used more widely by mission enablers seeking to determine the extent to which a church is involved in wholistic outreach.

The results of this research have suggested that the mission of the churches was being enhanced by parish nursing in three main ways:

1. In the parish nurse churches, ministry team-members and churchgoers spent more time on behalf of the church with people who did not attend church;

2. In the parish nurse churches people offered significant volunteering time around the health initiative;

3. In the parish nurse churches the range of missional activities undertaken by staff and congregation together was broadened, not only in the realm of physical health but across the board, in mental health, community health, and spiritual health interventions.

Other significant findings were that in all fifteen churches there was greater engagement with other voluntary and statutory bodies; that from the minister's perspective there was consensus that the mission work of their church had been enhanced by parish nursing, that both parish nurses and ministers were enthusiastic about the health ministry work that was being undertaken; and that there was evidence of an intrinsically integrated form of outreach taking place in the work of the parish nurse.

## THEMES FOR FURTHER RESEARCH

Eighteen months may allow both nurse and ministers to describe the difference parish nursing has made to their own practice, but it may not be enough to see the outcomes on the congregation as a whole, or on the lives of individuals that have been reached through the practice. Further research is needed to explore the long-term outcomes in these fifteen projects. The work described here was limited in that there were only seventy-seven churches with which the parish nurse churches were compared. This is too small a sample to be sure that there is consistency of representation in each of the different categories of size, denomination, and context. It would also be useful also to make comparisons by theological stance, although that may be difficult to define in an objective way.

It was noted in chapter 5 that in the US, parish nurses commonly work within congregations as part of the in-house pastoral care program rather than the mission program. It would be interesting to examine how the practice is different in the UK as a result of this contrast, and identify any implications for training and resourcing.

Another way of looking at parish nursing would be from the perspective of the client. Have they experienced any spiritual growth or other positive or negative effects through the ministry of the parish nurse? To this end a careful methodology that includes appropriate ethical considerations would need to be developed. A further proposal might examine perspectives on the value of the health ministry from other health providers or voluntary organizations in the same community, and whether or not this has influenced their own view of faith.

Research studies around the measurement of outcomes would help health providers to understand the value of a church's contribution, and may enable them to assess the effect of the spiritual care that they currently offer with greater clarity. It might also help churches to achieve more significant funding for their health ministry, which in turn may increase their mission activity. And research proposals that seek to identify the wholistic needs relating to specific age-groups or diseases would help parish nurses to be more effective in their practice.

All of the knowledge that is built up as a result of these and other health-related studies should be fed into the continuing education and training programs led by Parish Nursing Ministries UK, so that best practice in health care along with theological reflection form the trademarks of their future work.

## VISION

It is my hope that this work is simply the beginning of a larger research program that assists nurses, health providers, and churches to use their resources more effectively in their partnership with each other and with God in his mission to the world.

The vision held by PNMUK is that everyone who so chooses in the UK will eventually have access to a parish nurse. For this to happen, at least one church in every large village and town or district in the UK needs to have a parish nurse alongside and as a complement to health care provision. There are currently six hundred thousand registered nurses on the Nursing and Midwifery Council's register. If only 10 percent of them have any link to a local church that would mean there are sixty thousand nurses who could possibly become parish nurses. And there are just forty-six thousand churches in the UK.[1] PNMUK therefore believes that the vision is achievable.

PNMUK has developed a sustainable support structure, with training, professional networking, model policies, documentation, quality standards and resources that will supply each church with what is needed to engage in health ministry of this kind. The aim now is to promote the practice among nurses, and churches of all kinds so that many more may take up this challenge, and that there will be a continuous stream of nurses willing to take on this work when the current nurses move on or retire.

## IMPLEMENTATION

This study shows that the appointment of a parish nurse makes a difference to the mission of the local church. How may ministers and church leaders respond? In the experience of helping more than eighty churches to start a health ministry over the last few years, one of the key factors for a

1. Brierley, "Number of UK Churches."

successful and sustainable project has been the encouragement of the local church leader. Nurses are sometimes hidden members of the congregation, deeply engaged in their NHS work to the extent that their pattern of shifts may not enable them to take on much church responsibility. They may never have heard of parish nursing or understood the way in which it may complement and enhance NHS provision. Yet when a minister introduces the idea to them, there is often a positive response. If more churches are to take up parish nursing, ministers need to be on the lookout for nurses in their congregations, and to contact PNMUK for news of where they may visit a nearby project. They need to gather together the health professionals in their church and neighboring churches along with anyone interested in the project to pray, to research the local needs along with GP practices and other health providers, and consider possible responses. Can funding be raised for a paid post? Perhaps just for one or two days per week? If not, are there nurses already in the congregation(s) that are willing to form a team of volunteer nurses together? Most parish nurses work part time in the NHS in addition to their work for the church, but if they need to take a break for family reasons or are soon to retire, parish nursing, whether voluntary or paid, may provide enough hours, updating opportunities, and professional supervision to enable them to keep their nursing registration. PNMUK may be able to provide someone to come and talk with leadership teams and interested groups. One week training courses for the nurses and other health professionals are held three times a year. PNMUK provides this, along with ongoing coordination support, annual symposia and study days, resources for the nurses, model policies for the churches, ideas for finding funding, professional networking and advice. More information is available on their website www.parishnursing.org.uk.

If churches are able to re-discover a ministry of health alongside government provision, they will not only be engaging in the work of God's kingdom and acting in ways that are authentic to the gospel they proclaim, but they will also be helping to build the kind of society that allows for people to discover purpose for living, that offers choice, and that makes it possible for lives to be transformed. It is my hope that this book will contribute towards that aim.

# Appendix 1

## Letter of Introduction

Dear _____,

You may know that I am currently engaged in a professional doctorate study on health-related mission initiatives and I wonder if you would be kind enough to help me in my research.

This would involve the completion of the attached questionnaire. I may also ask for a one hour interview with you and possibly a one hour focus group with a few people from your congregation.

All questionnaires will be treated confidentially and kept in a locked filing cabinet. All participants may choose whether or not to answer any question put to them and whether or not to partake in the focus group. All participants will have a right to read the completed research work.

I would be very grateful for your assistance with this work and hope that the outcome will be of use to us all.

With warm greetings

# Appendix 2

## Pre-interview Survey Sent to Ministers

Church:_____

Denomination:_____

**A.**

1. Please circle context of church:

Rural village | Market Town | Urban City centre | Suburban commuter
Council housing estate | Other: please define_____

2. Please circle average attendance at weekly worship events:

10–49 | 50–99 | 100–149 | 150–199 | over 200

3. Please circle ethnicity of attenders:

mixed | majority black and ethnic | majority white

4. Age-range of average attenders at weekly worship events:

| Age range | 0–20 | 21–40 | 41–60 | 61–80 | 81+ |
|---|---|---|---|---|---|
| Average attendance | | | | | |

5.  Is the age/ethnicity of the attenders similar to that of the community with which the church seeks to engage?

Yes  |  No

6.  Does the church have a mission statement/strategy?

Yes  |  No  |  If yes, please attach a copy

7.  How many hours per week does your parish nurse work for the church?

Voluntary:                    | Paid:

8.  How long has s/he been in post?

9.  Has there been any kind of commissioning or recognition service?

Yes  |  No

10. Do you, the parish nurse and/or her volunteer team spend time working with/for with people who are not regular Sunday worship attenders? If yes, please circle the percentage of time spent in this way.

0–10% | 10–25% | 25–40% | 40–55% | 55-70% | 70–85% | 85–100%

11. Are there other health professionals in the church congregation who are employed with the NHS or private health care?

12. If yes, what support does the church offer them?

**B.**

Please tick which of these activities you (Min), the parish nurse (PN), or other members of the congregation (Co) have been involved in as part of the church's outreach within the last eighteen months.

|  | Min | PN | Co |
|---|---|---|---|
| 1. Abuse protection |  |  |  |
| 2. Active listening |  |  |  |
| 3. Advocacy: community |  |  |  |
| 4. Advocacy: individual |  |  |  |
| 5. Anxiety management |  |  |  |
| 6. Behavioural management |  |  |  |
| 7. Benefits advice |  |  |  |
| 8. Bereavement care |  |  |  |
| 9. Boundary-setting |  |  |  |
| 10. Caregiver support |  |  |  |

(This continued alphabetically with all the categories listed in Appendix 7)

Other: please include any activities that do not fit these categories.
Please star any of these activities where the parish nurse has made a significant contribution that you would be prepared to expand upon in a semi-structured interview.

(The first two pages of this survey were also used for the control sample of churches without a parish nurse but all references to the parish nurse were removed.)

## C.

Please insert your response to the following statements:

| | Strongly agree | Agree | Disagree | Strongly disagree |
|---|---|---|---|---|
| 1) I and/or my family have received advice for health as a result of the appointment. | | | | |
| 2) The number of people volunteering for activities has increased since the appointment. | | | | |
| 3) Our liaison with other voluntary bodies has increased since the appointment. | | | | |
| 4) I have seen some spiritual growth in people that the parish nurse has worked with i.) in those who attend church regularly | | | | |
| ii.) in those who do not. | | | | |
| 5) People have come to faith, partly as a result of a parish nurse intervention. | | | | |

| | | | | |
|---|---|---|---|---|
| 6) People have joined the church partly as a result of a parish nurse intervention. | | | | |
| 7) I have found it difficult to work with a parish nurse in my team. | | | | |
| 8) There have been irresolvable difficulties in relationships between the parish nurse and other church workers. | | | | |
| 9) I think that having a parish nurse has made no difference to our mission programme. | | | | |
| 10) The parish nurse has helped us increase our involvement in mission activities. | | | | |
| 11) I recommend that other churches appoint parish nurses to enhance their mission involvement. | | | | |

Thank you for completing this initial questionnaire.

The next stage of the research is to conduct a semi-structured hour-long interview with you and possibly an hour-long focus group. Ideally the focus groups will consist of a representative group of the congregation; at least some of them will have worked with or received help from the parish nurse. A consent form will be sent to you in advance so that the constituents of that group may choose whether or not to opt in to it and confidentiality will be assured.

Please could you indicate any days in June/July/August that you might be free for such an interview and focus group?

# Appendix 3

## Semi-structured Interview Questions: Ministers

**WELCOME**

Introduction to study and confidentiality precautions.

1. Can you tell me a bit more about this church and its community?
2. How long have you been working with this church?
3. What changes have you seen since you have been here?
4. What prompted you to think about having a parish nurse?
5. How did you come to the decision to go ahead with it?
6. How did you decide what activities she would concentrate on?
7. You starred a few items that you might want to expand on . . . do you want to do that now? (Or) Does your parish nurse have a particular strength?
8. Since the appointment of the parish nurse can you give me any examples of ways in which she or he interacts with regular church people?
9. How has this been received?

10. Since the appointment of the parish nurse, can you describe any ways in which she has engaged with people who don't come to church regularly?

11. How has this been received?

12. Have there been any particular challenges? How did you overcome them?

13. Do you foresee any future challenges?

14. Would you recommend the idea of having a parish nurse to other churches? If so, why?

# Appendix 4

## Semi-structured Interview Questions: Nurses

**WELCOME**

Introduction to study and confidentiality precautions.

1. What prompted you to think about being a parish nurse?
2. How did you come to the decision to go ahead with it?
3. How did you decide what activities you would concentrate on?
4. Do you have a particular strength?
5. Since your appointment can you give me any examples of ways in which you have interacted with regular church people? How has this been received?
6. Since your appointment, can you describe any ways in which you have engaged with people who don't come to church regularly? How this been received?
7. Has spiritual care featured in your work? If so, how?
8. Have there been any particular challenges? How did you overcome them?

9. Do you foresee any future challenges?

10. Would you recommend being a parish nurse to other nurses? If so why?

# Appendix 5

## Interventions by Category

### PHYSICAL HEALTH INTERVENTIONS:

B10, B19, B20, B24, B26, B30, B31, B32, B35, B36, B41, B42, B43, B48, B49, B52, B53, B54, B55, B64, B65.

Caregiver support, discharge planning, dying care, exercise promotion, first aid, health education, health screening, health system guidance, lifestyle management, medication management, nutritional counselling, oral health promotion, pain management, referral, risk assessment, self-care facilitation, relaxation therapy, skin care, smoking cessation/substance abuse, weight reduction assistance, foot care.

### MENTAL HEALTH INTERVENTIONS:

B1, B2, B5, B6, B8, B9, B11, B13, B14, B15, B18, B21, B29, B38, B61.

Abuse protection, active listening, anxiety management, behavioural management, bereavement and loss care, boundary setting, communication enhancement, conflict resolution, coping enhancement, counselling, decision-making support, emotional support, guilt work facilitation, memory loss care, support system enhancement.

## SOCIAL AND COMMUNITY HEALTH INTERVENTIONS:

B3, B4, B7, B12, B16, B17, B22, B23, B25, B27, B33, B34, B39, B40, B47, B50, B56, B60, B62, B63.

Advocacy, (individual and community), benefits/financial advice, complex relationship building, crisis intervention, cultural and interpretation issues, employment issues, end of life issues, family support, food /clothing provision, housing/home maintenance assistance, learning facilitation, case conferences, community networking, recreation therapy, security enhancement, socialisation enhancement, support group referral, volunteer coordination, volunteer support.


## SPIRITUAL HEALTH INTERVENTIONS:

B28, B37, B44, B45, B46, B57, B58, B59, B66, B67, B68

Forgiveness facilitation, meditation, pastoral care, prayer ministry, presence when words are inadequate, spiritual care and support, sacramental ministry, spiritual abuse protection, healing services, group discussions about faith, individual discussions about faith.

# Bibliography

Adams, G. "Nurses in Churches—Parish Nursing: Getting Body and Soul Back Together." *Kentucky Nurse* 41.3 (1993) 16–17.

Alderson, Andrew. "Nurse Suspended for Offering to Pray for Elderly Patients' Recovery." *Daily Telegraph.* January 31, 2009. http://www.telegraph.co.uk/health/healthnews/4409168/Nurse-suspended-for-offering-to-pray-for-patients-recovery.html.

Anderson, C. M. "The Delivery of Health Care in Faith-based Organizations: Parish Nurses as Promoters of Health." *Journal of Health Communication* 16.1 (2004) 117–28.

Benn, C., and E. Senturias. "Health, Healing and Wholeness in the Ecumenical Discussion." *International Review of Mission* XC, 18 (2001) 356–57.

Berger, Peter, et al. *Religious America, Secular Europe? A Theme and Variations.* Farnham, Surrey: Ashgate, 2008.

Bergquist, S., and J. King. "Parish Nursing—A Conceptual Framework." *Journal of Holistic Nursing* 12.2 (1994) 155–70.

Bickley, Lynda E. "The Contribution of Nursing to Health Care." MA diss., University of Wales, Swansea, 1995.

Biddix, V., and H. N. Brown. "Establishing a Parish Nursing Program." *Nursing and Health Care Perspectives* 20.2 (1999) 72–75.

Bokinskie, J. C., and P. K. Kloster. "Effective Parish Nursing: Building Success and Overcoming Barriers." *Journal of Christian Nursing* 25.1 (2008) 20–25.

Boland, C. S. "Parish Nursing: Addressing the Significance of Social Support and Spirituality for Sustained Health-promoting Behaviors in the Elderly." *Journal of Holistic Nursing* 16.3 (1998) 355–68.

Bolin, Joseph. "Pope John Paul II on Vocation." *Paths of Love.* http://www.pathsof love.com/johnpaul-vocation.html.

Bosch, D. *Transforming Mission: Paradigm Shifts in Theology of Mission.* New York: Orbis, 1993.

Boulton, J. "Welfare Systems and the Parish Nurse in Early Modern London, 1650–1725." *Family and Community History* 10.2 (2007) 127–51.

Brierley, Peter. *Pulling out of the Nosedive.* London: Christian Research, 2006.

———. "Number of UK churches." *Why Church.* http://www.whychurch.org.uk/num_churches.php.

Brown, Callum G. *The Death of Christian Britain.* Second ed. Oxford: Routledge, 2009.

Bruce, Steve. "The Demise of Christianity in Britain." in *Predicting Religion:Christian, Secular and Alternative Futures,* edited by Grace Davie, et al. Aldershot: Ashgate, 2003.

———. "Secularisation, Church and Popular Religion." *Journal of Ecclesiastical History,* 62.3 (2011) 543–61.

Brunton, D. *Health, Disease and Society in Europe 1800–1930: A Source Book.* Manchester: Manchester University Press, 2004.

Buechner, Frederick. *Wishful Thinking; A Theological ABC.* San Francisco: Harper San Francisco, 1993.

Buijs, R., and J. Olson. "Parish Nurses Influencing Determinants of Health." *Journal of Community Health Nursing* 18.1 (2001) 13–23.

Burkhart, L., et al. "Mapping Parish Nurse Documentation into the Nursing Interventions Classification: A Research Method." *Computers Informatics Nursing* 23.4 (2005) 220–29.

Burkhart, L., and P. A. Solari-Twadell. "Spirituality and Religiousness: Differentiating the Diagnoses through a Review of the Nursing Literature." *Nursing Diagnosis* 12.2 (2001) 45–54.

Cameron, David. "Transcript of a Speech by the Prime Minister on the Big Society." *Gov.uk.* July 19, 2010. http://www.number10.gov.uk/news/speeches-and-transcripts/2010/07/big-society-speech-53572.

Castledine, George. "The Spiritual State We're In: The Role of Parish Nursing." *British Journal of Nursing* 17.12 (2008) 803.

Chase-Ziolek, M., and J. Striepe. "A Comparison of Urban versus Rural Experiences of Nurses Volunteering to Promote Health in Churches." *Public Health Nursing* 16.4 (1999) 270–79.

Chesley, D. A."Parish Nursing & Cancer Prevention." *Texas Nursing* 72.6 (1998) 5.

Chester, Tim. *Good News to the Poor.* Nottingham: IVP, 2004.

"Church Health Check." *Livability.* http://www.livability.org.uk/landing.asp?id=12.

Church of England. "The Five Marks of Mission." *Anglican Communion.* http://www.anglicancommunion.org/ministry/mission/fivemarks.cfm.

———. *Mission-Shaped Church*: Church of England Mission and Public Affairs Council, 2004.

———. *A Time to Heal: Church of England Report on the Healing Ministry.* London: Church of England, 2000.

Christian Medical Fellowship. "The Engel Scale." *Christian Medical Fellowship.* http://www.cmf.org.uk/publications/content.asp?context=article&id=1288.

"Christian Nurse Suspended for Offering to Pray." *Nursing Times.* February 29, 2009. http://www.nursingtimes.net/a-christian-nurse-suspended-for-offering-to-pray-has-sparked-health-care-and-religion-debate/1997207.article.

Christus Rex. "Vatican II on Mission." *Christus Rex.* http://www.christusrex.org/www1/CDHN/v16.html

Chryssides, George. D., and Ron Geaves. *The Study of Religion: An Introduction to Key Ideas and Methods.* London: Continuum, 2007.

Clark, M. B., and J. K. Olson. "A Partnership that Matters: Collaborative Interdisciplinary Ministry among Parish Nurses and Faith Group Leaders." *Journal of Health Care Chaplaincy* 11.2 (2001) 27–40.

Clarke, J. "A Critical View of How Nursing has Defined Spirituality." *Journal of Clinical Nursing* 18 (2009) 1666–73.

"Code of Practice for Registered Nurses." *Nursing and Midwifery Council.* www.nmc.org. uk.

Daniels, Maureen. "World Forum Newsletter." *Church Heal Center.* http://www. parishnurses.org/DocumentLibrary/World%20Forum%20Newsletters/In%20 the%20World%20Forum--09-10.pdf.

Davie, Grace. *Religion in Britain since 1945: Believing Without Belonging.* Oxford: Blackwell, 1994.

Denscombe, Martyn. *The Good Research Guide, Second edition.* Maidenhead: Open University Press, 2003.

Department of Health. *Your Guide to the NHS.* London: HMSO, 2001.

————. "Religion or Belief: A Practical Guide for the NHS." *Gov.uk.* http://www.dh.gov. uk/prod_consum_dh/groups/dh_digitalassets/documents/digitalasset/dh_093132. pdf.

————. *Self-care: A Real Choice. Practical Examples for Self Care Support.* London: HMSO, 2005.

DePoy, E., and L. Gitlin. *Introduction to Research.* Saint Louis: Mosby, 1998.

Dewar, Francis. *Called or Collared.* London: SPCK, 2000.

Dingwall, R., et al. "Nurses and Servants." In *An Introduction to the Social History of Nursing.* London: Routledge, 2002.

Dyess, S., et al. "The State of Research for Faith Community Nursing." *Journal of Religion and Health* 49.2 (2010) 188–99.

"Engel Scale." *Christian Medical Fellowship.* http://www.cmf.org.uk/publications/content. asp?context=article&id=1288.

Engelsviken, T. "Missio Dei: the Understanding and Misunderstanding of a Theological Concept in European Churches and Missiology." *International Review of Mission* XCII 367 (2002) 481–97.

"The Faithworks Charter." *Faithworks.* September 11, 2014. http://www.faithworks.info/ Standard.asp?id=7432.

Fensham, Charles. "To be Sent: If Everything is Mission then Nothing is Mission." *Presbyterian Record.* June 1, 2008. http://www.presbyterianrecord.ca/2008/06/01/ to-be-sent/.

Feucht, Oscar E. *Everyone a Minister.* St Louis: Concordia, 1979.

Flett, John. G. *The Witness of God: The Trinity, Missio Dei, Karl Barth and the Nature of Christian Community.* Grand Rapids: Eerdmans, 2010.

Fytche, Jennie. "Parish Nursing as Christian ministry to Children in the UK." MA diss., University of Gloucestershire, 2010.

Gardner, R. B. "Vocation and Story: Biblical Reflections on Vocation." *Brethren Life and Thought* 46.3 (2001) 208–12.

Gallup. "Church Attendance USA 2002–2005." http://www.gallup.com/poll/22414/ Mormons-Evangelical-Protestants-Baptists-Top-Church-Attendance-List.aspx.

Gilbert, A. "Secularisation and the Future." In *A History of Religion in Britain: Practice and Belief from Pre-Roman Times to the Present,* edited by S. Gilley, and W. J. Sheils. Oxford: Blackwell, 1994.

Gilliat-Ray, S. "Nursing, Professionalism, and Spirituality." *Journal of Contemporary Religion* 18.3 (2010) 335–49.

Goldsmith, Martin. *Matthew and Mission: the Gospel through Jewish Eyes.* London: Paternoster, 2001.

## Bibliography

Glaser, B. G., and A. L. Strauss. *The Discovery of Grounded Theory: Strategies for Qualitative Research*. New York: Aldine de Gruyter Hawthorne, 1967.

Greasley, P., et al. "The Concept of Spiritual Care in Mental Health Nursing." *Journal of Advanced Nursing* 33.5 (2001) 629–37.

Gunther, W. "The History and Significance of World Mission Conferences in the 20th Century." *International Review of Mission* 92 (2003) 521–37.

Hadaway, C. K., and P. L. Marler. "Did You Really go to Church This Week?" *Religion Online*. May 6, 1998. http://www.religion-online.org/showarticle.asp?title=237.

Health Education Authority. *Mental Health Promotion: A Quality Framework*. London: Health Education Authority, 1997.

"A Health Visiting Timeline." *Unite the Union*. http://www.unitetheunion.org/pdf/150%20yr%20timeline%2025.4.12.pdf.

Heelas, Paul, and Linda Woodhead. *The Spiritual Revolution: Why Religion is Giving Way to Spirituality*. Oxford: Blackwell, 2005.

Hendriksen, W. *The Gospel of Matthew*. Edinburgh: Banner of Truth Trust, 1976.

"Historical Overview of Parish Nursing in Canada." *Canadian Association for Parish Nurse Ministry*. June 2010. http://www.capnm.ca/historical_overview.htm.

"History of the Kaiserswerth Diaconate," *Kaiserswerther Diakonie*. http:///www.kaiserswerther-diakonie.de.

H.M. Government. "National Statistics 2001." *Gov.uk*. http://www.statistics.gov.uk/pdfdir/religion1004.pdf.

Holy Trinity Brompton. "Besom: Sweep Away Suffering." http://www.besom.com/local-besoms.

Hurding, Roger F. *Pathways to Wholeness*. London: Hodder and Stoughton, 1998.

Johnson, B., et al. "Documenting the Practice." In *Parish Nursing: Promoting Whole Person Health within Faith Communities*, edited by Solari-Twadell, Phyllis Ann, and Mary Ann McDermott, 233–48. Thousand Oaks, CA: Sage, 1998.

Kirk, J. Andrew. *What is Mission? Theological Explorations*. London: Darton, Longman, and Todd, 1999.

Kleinhans, K. "The Work of a Christian Vocation in Lutheran Perspective." *Word and World* 25.4 (2005) 394–402.

Köstenberger, Andreas. "The Place of Mission in New Testament Theology." *Missiology: An International Review* 27.3 (1999) 347–62.

Köstenberger, Andreas, and Peter T. O'Brien. *Salvation to the Ends of the Earth*. Downers Grove, IL: IVP, 2004.

Kuhrt, Stephen. *Tom Wright for Everyone: Putting the Theology of N.T. Wright into Practice in the Local Church*. London: SPCK, 2011.

Lausanne Movement. "The Cape Town Commitment." In *The Third Lausanne Conference on World Evangelization*. Cape Town, South Africa: Lausanne Movement, 2011.

———. "The Manila Manifesto." www.lausanne.org/manila-1989/manila-manifesto.html.

Lorentzon, M. and J. Bryant. "Leadership in British Nursing: a Historical Dimension." *Journal of Nursing Management* 5 (1997) 271–78.

Lucas, Ernest, ed. *Christian Healing; What Can We Believe?* London: Lynx Communications, 1997.

Marshall, A. *A Kind of Life Imposed on Man: Vocation and Social Order from Tyndale to Locke*. Toronto: University of Toronto Press, 1996.

# BIBLIOGRAPHY

McDermott, M. A., and J. Burke. "When the Population is a Congregation: The Emerging Role of the Parish Nurse." *Journal of Community Health Nursing* 10.3 (1993) 179–90.

McDonald, Lynne. *Florence Nightingale at First Hand: Vision, Power, Legacy*. London: Continuum, 2010.

McGilvray, J. *The Quest for Health and Wholeness*. Tubingen: Christian Medical Commission, 1981.

McSherry, Wilfred. *Making Sense of Spirituality in Nursing and Health Care Practice*. London, Jessica Kingsley, 2008.

————. *Spirituality in Nursing Practice*. London: Churchill Livingstone, 2000.

"The Micah Network Declaration." *Micah Network*. http://www.micahnetwork.org/en/integral-mission/micah-declaration

Murray, Ruth, and Judith Proctor Zentner. *Nursing Concepts for Health Promotion*. London, Prentice Hall, 1989.

Murray, Stuart. *Church Planting, Laying Foundations*. Carlisle: Paternoster, 1998.

NHSTA Directory of Complementary and Alternative Practitioners, *NHS Trust Association*, "House of Lords Report on Complementary Medicine." http://www.nhsdirectory.org.

O'Brien, M. E. "Parish Nursing Meeting Spiritual Needs of Elders Near the End of Life." *Journal of Christian Nursing* 23.1 (2006) 28–33.

————. *Spirituality in Nursing: Standing on Holy Ground*. 3rd ed., Sudbury, MA: Jones and Bartlett, 2008.

Ogden, Greg. *The New Reformation: Returning the Ministry to the People of God*. Grand Rapids: Zondervan, 1990.

Paley, John. "Religion and the Secularisation of Health Care." *Journal of Clinical Nursing*, 18 (2009) 1963–74.

————. "Spirituality and Nursing: a Reductionist Approach." *Nursing Philosophy* 9 (2008) 3–18.

Patterson, Deborah L. *Health Ministries: A Primer for Clergy and Congregations*. Cleveland, OH: Pilgrim, 2008.

Peskett, Howard, and Vinoth Ramachandra. *The Message of Mission*. Nottingham: IVP, 2003.

Peterson, J. E., "Breaking the Cycle of School Violence: How Can Parish Nurses Help?" *Journal of Christian Nursing* 18.3 (2001) 20–23.

Plante, Thomas G., and Allen C. Sherman. *Faith and Health: Psychological Problems*. New York: Guilford, 2001.

Powell, W. R. "West Ham Philanthropic Institutions." *British History Online*. http://www.british-history.ac.uk/report.aspx?compid=42763.

Prochaska, Frank. *Christianity and Social Service in Modern Britain: The Disinherited Spirit*. Oxford: Oxford University Press, 2006.

Reed, P. G. "An Emerging Paradigm for the Investigation of Spirituality in Nursing." *Research in Nursing and Health* 15 (1992) 349–57.

Rethemeyer, A., and B. A. Wehling. "How are we Doing? Measuring the Effectiveness of Parish Nursing." *Journal of Christian Nursing* 21.2 (2004) 10–12.

Rian-Evans, Abigail. *Redeeming Marketplace Medicine: A Theology of Healthcare*. Cleveland, OH: Pilgrim, 1999.

Robinson, J. A. T. *The Body*. London: SCM, 1952.

Rouse, D. P. "Parish Nursing: a Community-based Pediatric Clinical Experience." *Nurse Educator* 25.1 (2000) 8–11.

Rydholm, L. "Patient-focused Care in Parish Nursing." *Holistic Nursing Practice* 11 (1997) 47–60.

Sacks, Jonathan. *The Home We Build Together.* London: Continuum, 2007.

Schwarz, C., and C. Schalk. *Natural Church Development Implementation Guide.* St Charles, IL: ChurchSmart Resources, 1998.

Scorer, C. G. *Healing, Biblical, Medical and Pastoral.* London: Christian Medical Fellowship, 1979.

Scott, L., and J. Sumner. "How do Parish Nurses Help People? A Research Perspective." *Journal of Christian Nursing* 10.1 (1993) 16–18.

Senior, Donald, and Carroll Stuhlmueller. *The Biblical Foundations for Mission.* London: SCM, 1983.

Sider, Ronald. *Rich Christians in an Age of Hunger.* London: Hodder and Stoughton, 1998.

Simpson, G. M. "A Reformation is a Terrible Thing to Waste." In *The Missional Church in Context,* edited by Craig Van Gelder, 75. Grand Rapids: Eerdmans, 2007.

Singlehurst, Laurence. *Sowing, Reaping, Keeping.* Leicester: Crossway, 1995.

Solari-Twadell, Phyllis Ann, et al. *Parish Nursing: The Developing Practice.* Park Ridge, IL: National Parish Nurse Resource Center, 1990.

Solari-Twadell, Phyllis Ann, and Mary Ann McDermott, eds. *Parish Nursing; Development, Education, and Administration.* Saint Louis: Elsevier Mosby, 2006.

———. *Parish Nursing: Promoting Whole Person Health within Faith Communities.* Thousand Oaks, CA: Sage, 1999.

Steuernagel, V. R. "Social Concern and Evangelization: the Journey of the Lausanne Movement." *International Bulletin of Missionary Research* 15 (1991) 53–56.

Stevens, R. Paul. *The Abolition of the Laity: Vocation, Work and Ministry in a Biblical Perspective.* Milton Keynes: Paternoster, 1999.

Stout, Geoffrey. *History of North Ormesby Hospital.* Cleveland, OH: Stout, 1989.

Swinton, John, and Harriet Mowat. *Practical Theology and Qualitative Research.* London: SCM, 2006.

Swinton, John, and Stephen Pattison. "Moving Beyond Clarity: Towards a Thin, Vague and Useful Understanding of Spirituality in Nursing Care." *Nursing Philosophy* 11 (2010) 22–37.

Thacker, Justin, and Marijke Hoek, eds. *Micah's Challenge: the Church's Responsibility to the Global Poor.* Milton Keynes: Paternoster 2008.

Thompson, P. E. "Between Text and Sermon: Jeremiah 1:1–10." *Interpretation* January (2008) 66–68.

Tuck, I., and D. C. Wallace. "Exploring Parish Nursing from an Ethnographic Perspective." *Journal of Transcultural Nursing* 11.4 (2000) 290–99.

Unruh, Heidi Rolland, and Ronald J. Sider. *Saving Souls, Serving Society.* Oxford: Oxford University Press, 2005.

Van Dover, L., and J. B. Pfeiffer. "Spiritual Care in Christian Parish Nursing." *Journal of Advanced Nursing* 57.2 (2006) 213–21.

Van Gelder, Craig. *The Ministry of the Missional Church.* Grand Rapids: Baker, 2007.

Vicedom, George F. *The Mission of God: An Introduction to the Theology of Mission.* Saint Louis: Concordia, 1965.

Wallace, D. C., et al. "Client Perceptions of Parish Nursing." *Public Health Nursing* 19.2 (2002) 128–35.

Warren, Robert. *The Healthy Churches' Handbook.* London: Church House, 2004.

Wearne, B. "Faith Community Nursing: Interview with Dr Anne Van Loon." http://www. freewebs.com/brucewearne/CommunityNursing1.pdf.

Weiss, D., et al. "Health Care Delivery in Faith Communities: the Parish Nurse Model." *Public Health Nursing* 14.6 (1997) 368–72.

"Who Are We?" *Fresh Expressions.* http://www.freshexpressions.org.uk/.

Wilkinson, John. *The Bible and Healing; a Medical and Theological Commentary.* Edinburgh: Handsel, 1998.

Wilson, Kim. "Do Christian Faith and Religious Practice Enhance the Coping Mechanisms of a Person with Chronic Illness?" BA diss., University of Wales, 2010.

Wimber, John, and Kevin Springer. *Power Healing.* London: Hodder and Stoughton, 1986.

Winkworth, C. *Life of Pastor Fliedner of Kaiserswerth:* London: Longman's, 1867.

Wordsworth, Helen A. "Parish Nursing—A Mission Opportunity for Local Churches in England." MTh diss., University of Wales, Spurgeon's College, 2001.

World Council of Churches. "The Healing Mission of the Church." In *Conference on World Mission and Evangelism.* Athens: World Council of Churches, 2004.

Wright, Christopher J. H. *The Mission of God: Unlocking the Bible's Grand Narrative.* Nottingham: IVP, 2006.

Wright, Tom. *Surprised by Hope* London: SPCK, 2007.

———. *Matthew for Everyone, Part 2.* London: SPCK, 2004.

Zersen, D. "Parish Nursing: 20th Century Fad?" *Journal of Christian Nursing* 11.2 (1994) 19–20.

10753584R00116

Printed in Great Britain
by Amazon.co.uk, Ltd.,
Marston Gate.